THE
ONE PAN
GOURMET

THE
ONE PAN
GOURMET

Fresh Food on
the Trail

DON JACOBSON

Ragged Mountain Press
Camden, Maine

Published by Ragged Mountain Press

10 9 8 7 6

Library of Congress Cataloging-in-Publication Data
Jacobson, Donald.
    The one pan gourmet: fresh food on the trail / Don Jacobson.
       p. cm.
    Includes index.
    ISBN 0-07-032123-X
    1. Outdoor cookery. 2. Camping—Equipment and supplies.
I. Title
TX823.J34 1993
641.5'78—dc20   93-20071
    CIP

Questions regarding the content of this book should be addressed to:

Ragged Mountain Press
P.O. Box 220
Camden, ME 04843

Questions regarding the ordering of this book should be addressed to:

The McGraw-Hill Companies
Customer Service Department
P.O. Box 547
Blacklick, OH 43004
Retail Customers: 1-800-262-4729
Bookstores: 1-800-722-4726

A portion of the profits from the sale of each Ragged Mountain Press book is donated to an environmental cause.
The One Pan Gourmet is printed on 60-pound Renew Opaque Vellum, an acid-free paper that contains 50 percent recycled waste paper (preconsumer) and 10 percent postconsumer waste paper.

Printed by R.R. Donnelley, Crawfordsville, Indiana.
Design by Joyce C. Weston.
Production by Molly Mulhern.
Edited by Jonathan Eaton, Kathleen C. Newman.

CONTENTS

Author's Note

As written, the recipes in this book serve one person generously. One is, after all, the least common denominator. If you're cooking for two, you can adjust most of the recipes simply by doubling the main ingredients (meats, vegetables, liquids, etc.) and increasing the spices sparingly. The same approach works for larger groups, although you need not triple or quadruple the meat portions to serve three or four. Taking 6 ounces as a single meat serving, 15 ounces will do for three people and 18 will feed four if you bump up the vegetables, sauces, and side dishes to fill the empty spaces.

The cookware recommended in Chapter 2 will feed one or two, but for larger groups you'll want a larger (10- to 12-inch) fry pan and a two-quart pot. And the oven alone will not suffice for larger groups; you could cook the meat portions in it, but you won't have room for the vegetables. On the other hand, more people mean more backpacks to carry cookware, so it all works out.

Finally, writing this book has taught me what personal expressions cooking and eating are. My biases and preferences are reflected throughout—it could be no other way. For example, I am fussy enough about cooking oils to carry small portions of four kinds (vegetable, olive, peanut, and corn) into the wilderness when my weekend menu calls for them. And I'm an omnivore. I like meat as much as vegetables, and my meals usually include both. Still, there are some delicious vegetarian recipes here (see the index), and a protein complementation chart (page 26) to reinforce the fact that outdoor adventures and vegetarianism are *not* incompatible. I hope you vegetarians won't be disappointed.

Acknowledgments

Just as in advertising, there's probably nothing in cooking that hasn't been tried a thousand times before. I have to tip my culinary hat to all those enterprising cooks who, over the years, have tried to brighten the insides of their friends, families, and neighbors.

The reader, especially if an experienced cook, will find that many of the recipes are old favorites presented with a slight twist. And that's the intent of this little work—to give a new look to campsite and trail cooking.

Many people have contributed to the recipes in this book, usually by testing them. The young men of Boy Scout Troop 80 in Downers Grove, Illinois, and the members of the Old Turkey patrol, especially dedicated Wood Badge Scouter Jim Baldwin, have been most eager and gracious in this respect. Other folks, such as Toby Erickson, an interpreter at the Charles L. Sommers National High Adventure Base (Boy Scouts of America), showed me that there are many who love to eat in the outdoors.

The lion's share of my gratitude, however, goes to three people who have encouraged my cooking efforts more than any others. To my father and mother, who taught me how to take the offerings provided by a teacher's pay and turn them into daily feasts; and to my wife, Pam, whose comments have helped keep me honest and who always urges me to create new non-microwave recipes for our table, I say thank you.

It is all those hikers and campers on the trails of New Hampshire, Illinois, and California who deserve the final credit. These hardy folks give me continued pleasure when I meet and learn from them among the trees and mountains of our country's wilderness.

This book is for you, if you've ever made camp with nothing more inspiring than the prospect of a can of beans or a hotdog to put the edge on your appetite. Read on, and eat well.

Downers Grove, Illinois
January, 1993

INTRODUCTION

No one has ever accused me of missing a meal intention-
ally. In fact, sometimes my girth has gotten in the way of
friendships, relationships, even the sun on the beach.

Oh, I'm not obese or even pleasingly plump. There's just
some extra padding on my frame that could—should—be
taken off for health's sake.

And that's one reason I camp, hike, take day outings,
and generally sweat, grunt, and groan my way up the
White Mountains, across the Angeles Crest, and back
down the Berkshires. And it's why I canoe the Boundary
Waters. I simply can't think of a better way to work off
unwanted lard than by burning it up in the company of
good friends and Mother Nature.

Funny thing is, the more you walk, paddle, or pedal, the
more calories you burn and the hungrier you get. The
hungrier you are, the more you want to eat. And that, as
the Bard put it, is the rub.

Hiking, biking, canoeing, kayaking, and camping are
emotional as well as physical experiences that should
leave the soul as refreshed as the body is exhausted. Over
my quarter century of clambering around this nation's
backroads, hills, and mountains, I have learned that the
visual and tactile pleasures of hiking—grand though they
be—are not the totality of the outdoor experience.

Think about this for a moment: On the trail, you wake
up about 6:30 or 7:00 in the morning. You eat. You pack
your gear and start walking.

Along the way, you see towering crags, sweeping vistas,

hawks, songbirds, alpine lakes . . . and the cares of your
workaday world fade into the recesses of your mind, and
eventually out of it altogether.

Then you stop to eat.

Back on the trail at 1:00, you point out the mountain lau-
rel or pinyon pines, talk about the condition of the trail
and your feet, and start looking closely at the distance you
have to cover before setting up camp that night. Why?
Because you want to be sure you'll have enough daylight
left to cook dinner.

Getting to the site, you pitch your tent, roll out your
sleeping bag, break out your cooking gear and food, and
concoct dinner.

Then you eat.

Maybe before turning in after an evening's storytelling,
you have a snack or a drink. Have you picked up a consis-
tent theme here?

On the average backpacking trip, hiker/campers really
do three basic things: They sleep. They hike. They eat.
And paddlers and pedalers are no different.

With rest breaks included, the most you can spend on
the trail without absolutely killing yourself is about nine
hours or so. If you average an hour or two for making and
breaking camp, and a generous 10 hours of sleep, that still
leaves about four hours for cooking, eating, and related
activities.

Nearly 30 percent of your waking hours are spent in
camp considering how to replace the calories you worked
off.

So don't tell me you want to kick back, boil some water,
and feast on a freeze-dried brick called Chicken Gumbo so
you can save preparation time.

Consider the alternative—something fresh, with crisp
green vegetables, a succulent sauce, and that toothsome,
satisfying, filling feeling only real food can give. Perhaps a
nice dessert. Something to be savored, not tolerated.
Something that encourages companions to linger over the

evening meal and the ensuing conversation. Something that soothes the digestion, improves your outlook, chases away the gloom of an unwelcome rainstorm, and requires a whole lot less water to prepare than the freeze-dried alternatives.

The simple fact is that all too many outdoorspeople have been brainwashed into thinking that, along with their high-tech sleeping bag, tent, stove, boots, and other gear, they have to spend immense amounts of money for high-tech food in order to save weight. Unless your trips are measured in weeks rather than days, it simply isn't so.

The human race managed nicely for more than 5,000 years of recorded history without freeze-dried foods. (I do bow to parched corn and beans, however.) Hannibal crossed the Alps without beef stew in a bag. Lindbergh crossed the Atlantic on a couple of ham sandwiches.

So take charge of your stomach. You, too, can eat the way you like in the outdoors. Grab your frying pan, your pot, or your oven, and live the one-pan lifestyle!

A PHILOSOPHY OF EATING

It seems there are only two schools of thought when it comes to eating in the backcountry. Either you're cooking out of the trunk of your car on a multiburner stove stoked by a limitless supply of white gas, or you're a minimalist subsisting on dried fruit and freeze-dried pouch food. But in the first case you're not really in the backcountry, and in the second case, in my opinion, you're not really eating.

I'll not take issue with my comrades of the high ranges and wilderness rivers who depend so heavily on freeze-dried foods. To cut their supply line for weeks at a time, they must compromise between comfort and convenience. So they pack a bunch of expensive foil packs, a lot of water, and an extra roll of toilet paper.

I don't camp out of my car except on rare occasions. That eliminates the 12-gallon cooler and crown roasts of lamb. Yet I reject the premise that you have to become an ascetic to enjoy the aesthetics of the great outdoors. Since I don't often spend more than two nights on the trail, I don't need to focus on component weight as much as the long-haul hikers and wilderness trippers do. And I sure don't need to drop five bucks a meal for something that, when ready, does not resemble food.

DIET AT HOME . . . EAT ON THE TRAIL

You need calories when you are on the trail. No matter how fit you are or how much you weigh, you are going to burn a few thousand calories to power the engine that drives you up hill and down dale. It doesn't make sense to skimp when it comes to eating. Three squares means three squares plus snacks to stoke the fires between meals. A decent breakfast will get you up and going faster than any dash of ice water and will keep you going longer. Lunch can be a little lighter if you want, but try to hit the four basic food groups. Fruit is important: Apples, pears, and peaches are Mother Nature's no-need-to-cook, ready-to-eat convenience foods. Stuff one or two in a side pocket in your pack. Grab and munch anytime. They're biodegradable and leave no nasty plastic wrappers to carry out.

Then there's dinner. The end of the day. The pinnacle of the hiking experience. Again, balance and variety should be the watchwords.

In the 25 years I've been hiking, I've learned that although you can get calories from almost anything, it's much more fun if you take the time to plan genuinely good meals. The happiest campers I've seen are the ones with full bellies. It doesn't matter if those stomachs are hidden inside hyperactive 11-year-olds or weighing down office-bound children of the '60s. Fill them up and there are smiles. Leave them empty and the growls will drown out even the mosquitoes. Fill them up with delicious fresh food and the planets will align and the music of the heavenly spheres will become audible.

I believe the time you spend in camp can and should be just as rewarding as the time spent walking. And a major part of that time ought to involve food preparation. As far as I'm concerned, it's not drudgery to add freshly sliced veggies to a broth shimmering around a couple of succulent chops. In fact, I savor those moments as much as a scenic vista graced by the widespread wings of a single peregrine.

You need not be bent over the stove continuously for two or three hours. Good food should be left to itself, to blend its flavors, work its magic in secrecy. With the prep work out of the way and the food in the pot, pan, or oven, take a few minutes to organize yourself for dinner. Clean up. Read. Tighten the tent ropes. Darn a sock. Grab a camera and shoot the sights around you.

Then you can eat the way the French intended—taking your time, digging into something that is really there, and appreciating the fact that you cooked it. What you are doing, of course, is paying yourself the ultimate compliment: that you do deserve to live well.

A QUESTION OF BALANCE: HARDWARE OR MUNCHWARE?

Even for the weekend backpacker, enjoyment varies inversely with the weight of the pack. The heavier your sack, the less fun you'll have.

One of the reasons your pack may be too heavy is that you are trying to bring all the comforts of home when you should be thinking about blending into the scenery as much as possible. I'm talking about low-impact camping.

Low-impact camping is a philosophy best embodied in the catch phrase, "Take nothing but pictures; leave nothing but footprints." It's that simple. People should not be outsiders when outdoors. They should become part of the picture, deemphasizing their individuality and perceived importance in the face of Creation's grandeur.

Entire books are devoted to this subject. For my money, The National Outdoor Leadership School's *Wilderness Guide* by Simer and Sullivan (Simon & Schuster, 1983, 1985) offers the best discussion about all aspects of living outdoors. After you've done it for a few years, loading up your backpack and eliminating excess fripperies and weight becomes a habit, not a conscious thought process.

Certain things you simply cannot do without when it comes to camping. Most of what you have to take along involves housing—tent, ground cloth, rainfly, tent stakes, and hatchet. (This is particularly true in the wet and buggy East. Eastern campers are always amazed the first time they sleep under the stars in the West and are not tormented by mosquitoes all night.) Of course, you'll also need your sleeping bag, sleeping pad, and, if you remember, pillow.

Add your survival and first-aid gear, spare clothes, bug repellent, toilet paper, extra line, and water, and you've got the makings of a load. To cover my own needs, I carry at least 3 quarts of water in my pack. No, not a quart per day. I fill up my bottles before I leave home. With a little luck, the water will last through to the next evening.

How about a deck of cards, a book, camera, film? We've got a lot in our pack, but not one bit of food. Where are we going to find room?

Simple question: Which is more important? Food or metal?

Food? Good, you can walk on my trail anytime.

If you have limited space but don't want to sacrifice the amount or type of food, that leaves only two items to cut: the stove (sure) or the cookware.

Over time I've learned that you never use every pot you carry. So I've eliminated most of the hardware provided in cook kits from my pack. I keep the cup, and I have a little teapot for boiling coffee water. But the frying pan, the small pot, and the big pot have become redundant.

We're not saving a lot of weight here, maybe a pound on the outside. But we are saving space. A frying pan tucks into the corner of the pack behind a tent or under some socks. A pot nestles on top of a stove or holds more clothes. If you bring but one pan or pot, you'll save valuable space. And, you'll challenge yourself to create interesting menus that take full advantage of that one pan.

And isn't that what trekking is all about? Challenging yourself to walk that extra mile? Climb that higher mountain? Impress yourself and your family or friends with your culinary wisdom on the trail?

I have spent the last decade or so cooking out of one pan. Usually, the smells and tastes are only for me, but every once in a while I share my efforts with somebody else who ends up bringing something different to the party. Maybe it's a new recipe for chili. Maybe it's a hot drink I've never tried.

This sharing of hospitality is traditional on the trail, as

fitting as Jimmy Stewart offering a cup of coffee to a grizzled stranger coming in out of the howling wastes. Food builds a bond, if only for a few hours, between people sharing a common, though separate, experience.

I've never had a problem building something that feeds two out of only one frying pan or stew pot. And usually that something brings a smile and, once in a while, a hand or two of gin rummy.

Even if you never simplify your camping kitchen to include just one pan, the fostering in your heart of the emotion that exemplifies one-pan hospitality will warm your spirit more than the finest Bordeaux.

THE PORTABLE KITCHEN

If you're planning to be a wilderness chef, you'll need a kitchen that lets you pursue culinary quests without enormous effort. With green trees or a rich blue sky as a canopy, you should be enjoying the aromas and tastes of your creations, not cursing a cracked cutting board or missing measuring spoons. Remember, good cooking can't be done without the right equipment.

As suggested in the last chapter, the fewer pieces of kitchen hardware you carry, the better. Give me a tablespoon measure, a Sierra cup (see photo on page 8), the palm of my hand, a sharp knife, and a piece of oak plank and I'll be happy as a pig in a corn crib. Of course, there are times when a few extra goodies make a pleasant difference. But let's stick to basics. They'll do the job, and they're lighter, too.

UTILITARIAN UTENSILS

Twenty-five years ago the state of the art in camping gear was stainless steel. It didn't rust, lasted forever, and weighed a ton. Christmas 1964 was my first as a Boy Scout, and I got everything, including a Scout fork, knife, and spoon set. The plastic carrying case has long since melted in some forgotten fire, but the three pieces of heavy metal are still slicing bacon, spearing chicken chunks, and stirring coffee. Stainless steel utensils remain a reasonable choice.

The technology of the '80s has given us utensils made of

Lexan, a polycarbonate material that is incredibly durable (though not flame- or heatproof) and lightweight. Other plastics—such as bottles, vials, and tubes to carry spices, condiments, and oils—have also lightened the camper's load.

I recently came across something called the "Outdoor Kitchen," manufactured by Outdoor Research. It crams everything you need into a compact carrying case: a fork/knife/spoon set, a large spoon, a spatula, measuring spoons, and a miniwhip—as well as a spice rack of salt and pepper, oils, grated cheese, and any number of liquids and powders. Everything is in one easy-to-find case rather than scattered around various pockets in your pack.

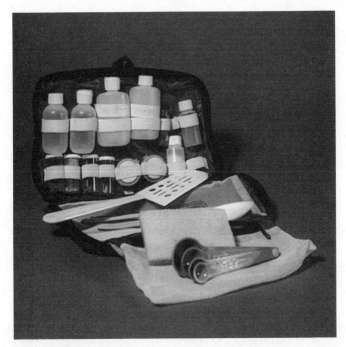

The outdoor kitchen.

Still life: Sierra cup, cutting board, potgrabs, waterbottle, utensils.

Add to this a cutting board, hot-pot tongs (potgrabs), pot holder, plate, Sierra cup or equivalent (for coffee, oatmeal, scooping servings out of a pot, etc.), and carving knife, and you have a basic field kitchen.

Of course, you don't have to buy a special (and potentially expensive) outfit. All you have to do is assemble the equipment with which you feel most comfortable. The accompanying table provides a brief checklist.

Most of the items can be packed in a few drawstring bags. Put the stove (more about that later), fuel, funnel, and hot-pot tongs in one bag. And don't forget the matches. In fact, bring several packs or boxes of waterproof matches and scatter them throughout your pack and clothing.

Waterproofing matches is something every Scout knows how to do. For those of you who missed this fun recreational activity, here's how you do it: In a double boiler (if you don't own one, float a one-pint saucepan in a one-quart pot about half full of water), melt some paraffin.

FIELD KITCHEN CHECKLIST

Personal Gear

Fork, knife, spoon   Metal cup
Plate or bowl   Water bottle

Kitchen Hardware

Hot-pot tongs or potgrabs   Pot holder
Cutting board (a piece of 1" x 4" x 8" oak will do)
Coffee/tea pot   Frying pan or pot
                                           (pick one)
Backpacking stove   Extra fuel in sealed
                                           container
Funnel for fuel   Waterproof matches
Spatula   Nested teaspoon/table-
                                           spoon measures
Large knife   Aluminum foil
Miniwhip   Backpacking oven
                                           (optional)
Trash bag   3 or 4 metal tent stakes
Liquid soap   Steel wool scrub pad

Kitchen Software

Seasonings/spices: Packed in plastic vials or other unbreak-
able containers. An excellent alternative is a 7-day pill box.
Label with white adhesive tape. Another possibility is the
plastic canisters used to store 35mm film. Label clearly.

Salt   Pepper   Sugar
Onion flakes Garlic powder   Celery salt
Hot sauce   Cajun spices   Seasoned salt
Basil   Thyme   Marjoram
Bay leaf   Paprika   Oregano
Parmesan cheese
Other spices (depending on recipes selected)
Instant or real coffee
Tea bags
Bouillon cubes
Vegetable, olive, peanut, and/or corn oils (pack as needed
for recipes selected) in 4-oz. containers

**Never melt the wax over direct heat. It could flame sud-
denly, causing serious burns.** Bundle about 10 wooden
kitchen matches with heavy thread and, holding the tail of
the thread, dip the heads and about one inch of the
matches into the wax. Remove and let cool to harden.
Voila! Waterproof matches!

Put the rest of your gear into other bags or pack pockets
as you deem appropriate. I like to keep it all together in
one easy-to-find place. There's nothing worse than your
piping-hot coffee turning to lukewarm mud while you
rattle through the pack looking for the sugar.

A FEW THOUGHTS ABOUT WATER

Trekkers have to contend with water availability wher-
ever they travel, and water quality is of even greater con-
cern. One way around the issue is to carry all your water,
but you need several quarts per person per day just to
avoid dehydration. Since water weighs 7-plus pounds per
gallon, the equation is certainly not in your favor even on
short trips. There's no way around relying on local
sources to keep your water bottles full.

And that means purifying the water you plan to drink
or use in cooking in order to kill off bacteria and other
nasty critters. That's easily accomplished by adding
chlorine tablets or iodine crystals, tablets, or liquid
(which most experts agree to be superior to chlorina-
tion), or by boiling the water for 5 to 10 minutes. You
can filter out silt and solid matter by pouring the water
through a handkerchief or other cloth strainer before
purification.

Iodine or chlorine treatment, however, imparts an
unpleasant taste to the water (commonly counteracted
with Kool-Aid or some such powdered drink mix), and
boiling is often impractical because it takes time and fuel.
There is a newer method of purification that replaces
chemicals or boiling and even surpasses them in one

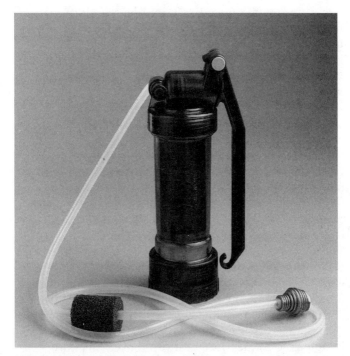

MSR Waterworks filter. Courtesy REI.

important respect: combating the nasty microbe named *Giardia lamblia. Giardia* is a hard-shelled microorganism that *usually* succumbs to boiling and chlorine or iodine purification methods. It lives in your lower gastrointestinal tract and does its best to make your life miserable for many, many months. You won't know if the water you're using is infested for 7 to 10 days, so "usually" is not good enough in my book.

The best way to deal with *Giardia* is to use a water filtration system. There are several on the market, with prices ranging up to $200 or more. All enable you to take water directly from almost any source and remove *Giardia*, bacteria, and other objectionable things. According to

Recreational Equipment (REI), a leading outdoor equipment manufacturer and retailer, some of the most important features to consider are removable filters, quality of
pump manufacture, output, and speed of filtration.

Remember to look at the filter porosity size, and make
sure it is less than 1 micron (0.2 micron is exceptional).
Giardia is somewhat smaller than 1 micron and has the
ability to squeeze through filter screens smaller than the
creature's actual diameter.

There is one exception to the absolute need to filter for
Giardia. If you're canoeing or boating in a lake and can get
more than 100 feet offshore into water that is 20 or more
feet deep, you can dip your pot with a greater degree of
confidence. The reason is that *Giardia* has a hard shell and
is relatively heavy for its size, so it sinks to the bottom.
This means that the traditionally accepted place for good
water—a bubbling stream or at the base of a crystalline
waterfall—is a big no-no unless you are carrying a decent
filtration system. The bottom is constantly being roiled,
keeping *Giardia* in circulation.

If you'd like to learn more about water purification and
filtration techniques, I suggest you consult an informative
pamphlet published by REI: "Water Purification FYI" is
available at any of REI's retail stores across the country.
You can also mail your request for this flyer to Recreational Equipment, Inc., Public Affairs Department, P.O.
Box 1938, Seattle, WA 98390.

PROMETHEUS, THE CAMPER

The key to good camp cooking is an excellent heat source.

Ancient Greeks and Romans, as well as more contem-
porary Pilgrims and Conestoga settlers, enjoyed a bounti-
ful supply of wood and a low ecological consciousness. A
roaring fire was part of every campsite. Seared meat,
either over- or undercooked breads, and enough soot and
ash to make any Gothamite proud were the rule.

But consider these facts before pulling out your axe or saw.

- An open fire is not a particularly efficient way to cook any-thing short of a steer on a spit. Even then, you had better like your meat blood-red rare or shoe-leather well done.
- Backpackers can't afford to participate in denuding our forests or adding the impact of an open fire to an envi-ronment already stressed to the maximum. Smoke and soot from your fire just heap insult upon the injury caused by factories and cars hundreds of miles to the west of that forest or just upstream from that beautiful gorge. And the next hikers to pass that way won't enjoy the sight of your fire ring any more than they would the sight of a beer can or a strand of pink toilet paper in the forest litter.
- The Forest Service has better things to do than put out wildfires caused by careless campers.

Since the late 1950s compact backpacking stoves pio-neered by the mountain-climbing fraternity have been available through many high-quality outfitters. Over the years the fuels of choice have varied from kerosene to white gas, butane, or propane. All have advantages and disadvantages.

Propane and butane ignite readily and provide instant heat, but are packaged in metal cartridges that add weight and must be carried back out of the wilderness.

Kerosene (diesel fuel) is readily available around the world, so if you're planning to travel overseas, a kerosene-burning stove might be the answer. Kerosene is difficult to light, however, and the quality of the fuel can vary from location to location. Pack a strainer—seriously—to remove the larger particles of debris from the distillate. Otherwise you'll clog the jets in your stove instantly, putting you and your comrades on a forced diet.

The most popular fuel for one-burner backpacking stoves is white gas—Coleman fuel. Available in camping supply stores, convenience marts, and gas stations, white gas ignites readily in cold or hot weather, providing opti-mum heat production.

Alcohol stoves are more popular in Europe than North America. I haven't used one, so I can't comment on their cooking qualities. But alcohol is less volatile than white gas and burns cooler, so you might want to cook your meals a bit longer than the recipes suggest.

I own four backpacking stoves, reflecting my history of cooking. My first, dating from the late '60s, was a Bleuet butane stove. Fueled by GAZ cartridges, this item let me cook without totally destroying my food. The cartridges lasted about an hour and weighed about 6 ounces each.

Then I got an Optimus white-gas wonder. This little blowtorch boils water in 7 minutes or less. Balancing a frying pan on the puny windscreen is a chore, which is why the kitchen list on page 9 includes tent stakes. Simply drive the stakes into the ground or snow, place the stove between them, and settle your pot on top.

The only problem with the Optimus (and similar stoves) is that the fuel tank is not pressurized. To get the fuel flowing, you have to prime the stove by dribbling a little white gas into the well at the base of the burner stem on top of the tank. Then you open the valve and light the priming fluid. There's no big flash or anything, but it tends to get messy. I've never been able to pour fuel *only* in the well, so I always end up with some on the tank or ground. (Note that I said "ground," not "floor." In every mountaineering film, the hardy souls perched at Camp V on the shoulder of Everest, melting snow for soup, are inside their tents. They have no choice. Either they cook in the tent or they starve. Outside they'd freeze solid before they could boil a cup of water. The trade-off is that they could burn to death inside their nylon tents in the event of a stove accident. No amount of food or cup of coffee is worth making that trade. Never cook in your tent.)

I also own a propane-powered stove. It's very compact and lightweight, but it has the same problems as the Bleuet.

Now I cook on a Coleman Peak One. There's a pump (like the one on a Coleman lantern) to pressurize the tank;

Fire power: The Coleman Peak One, left, and the Optimus.

the stove is self-priming. And the burner head is wide and sturdy enough to support an 8-pound Dutch oven holding a 5-pound roast with all the spuds, onions, and carrots you want. I've done it—and fed eight adults in the process. The stove doesn't weigh much and burns white gas.

Coleman also makes a Peak One that can use a variety of fuels. So for those of you heading where you never know what type of fuel you'll encounter next. . . .

POT, NOT HEAD, BANGERS

My goal when I pack is to cut the weight of the cooking gear to make room for extra-special fresh foodstuffs. So I'm careful what pots and pans I select to execute one-pan meals.

The truth is, you have to compromise. I'm a big fan of cast-iron pans, and at home I've got a skillet that's taken me about three years to break in just right. It cooks everything from bacon to cacciatore and weighs 12 pounds, which might as well be 100 from a backpacker's perspective. When my feet hit the trail, Old Faithful gets to rest in the cupboard.

The same thing goes for my Calphalon soup kettle. When you're walking, you simply can't afford even one pan that's going to put a dent in your shoulders and a crick in your back.

I tend to think aluminum when I travel the high country. It's light, fairly durable (though it will corrode), and reasonably priced. You're not going to cry too much if your aluminum 10-inch frying pan's handle breaks. You won't get too exercised if your one- or two-quart boiler springs a leak or picks up a ding or two. You'll just hie yourself off to the nearest discount store and invest another $6 to $10 for a replacement.

One nice thing about aluminum is that it heats up quickly and cools off just as fast. Also, a good inexpensive aluminum frying pan with one of the new nonstick surfaces makes cleanup easier. But the most salient advan-

Frying pans and potgrabs, best friends.

tage of aluminum is that it's lightweight. Some campers fear the possible long-term health risks of ingesting aluminum, which has even been linked to Alzheimer's disease, and mostly for that reason outdoor stainless steel cookware has made a comeback. Without doubt, the stainless steel is more durable, but the extra weight and expense keep me away from it. The most recent report I've read (November 1992) casts doubt on the connection between aluminum in the brain cells and Alzheimer's. For the short periods of time I'm on the trail, it's a risk I accept.

Incidentally, I just commented that you could replace your frying pan if you broke the handle. Actually, I think you should consider cutting the handle off from the get-go. When you're cooking over a single burner on less than even ground, a handle can throw everything off-balance. That's why you should pack hot-pot tongs, also known as potgrabs. They are your handle. Besides, factory-issue pot handles come loose, crack, melt, fall apart, and generally make packing your backpack a pain in the neck. They always seem to be jabbing into something—your poncho, your tent, or your spine.

As for which pot to include in your one-pan kit, I've found that the one-quart pot from my Mirro personal cook kit fills the bill quite nicely if I'm cooking for myself or one other person. It's well crafted, with a wide-bail handle. Instead of a regular top, I usually use a piece of foil.

Actually, any one-quart pot or kettle will do. If you have to, you can use a two-quart vessel. It doesn't weigh much more, and when packed away, the space inside will easily store your stove, fuel bottle, and a few other essentials.

One way to locate some of this hardware is through a store that carries or specializes in Boy Scouts of America equipment. It handles or has access to replacement parts for the big cook kits that Scout troops use (the Eight-Man Cook Kit) in abundance. The boys frequently lose one or two parts to a kit, and the adults usually end up finding

Going to pot.

replacements. One of those parts is a one-quart pot with top—perfect for a one-pan camper!

RAMPANT AMBITION . . . A ONE-PAN OVEN

Most backpackers can live happily ever after eating from a frying pan or a pot, but there are some who want more. These farsighted individualists realize that a world of casseroles, pies, and other delights awaits those willing to try something a bit off the wall . . . the one-pan oven.

I own three ovens suitable for backpacking or trekking. Of these, two were purchased—one for 50 cents, the other for $40. Either the Outback Oven or the no-longer-manu-

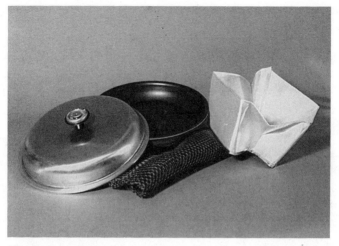

The Outback Oven.

factured Mirro model does the job, whether it's a roast or rolls.

If you haven't figured it out by now, I'm a very economical person . . . ah, what the . . . a cheapskate. So I've

The one-pan oven.

found a way to put together an oven at a good price—like darn near nothing.

An oven—whether fired by gas, wood, electricity, or cow chips—cooks by convection. No direct heat is applied to the food. Rather, the environment inside the oven is warmed sufficiently to raise the temperature of the food placed inside so that it cooks. The key is creating a current of hot air (convection) inside the oven to evenly distribute the heat throughout the cooking chamber. The second requirement is keeping the food off any surface in direct contact with the heat source.

A homemade cooking chamber is easy to construct. All you have to do is drink a lot of coffee, because that way you'll have an empty 3-pound can. You may have to visit a restaurant or commercial food broker, though. Most "three pounders" at your grocery are 39 ounces, not 48, and a 39-ounce can may be too small.

Once you have the can, a serviceable one-pan oven is just two easy steps away.

Step #l: Drill vent holes in the side of the can at the top and bottom. Using a ¼-inch drill, cut five or six holes around the perimeter of the can just below the top rim (the open end) and another five or six just above the bottom rim (the closed end) of the can. This allows air to enter and exit the oven as hot air rises from the bottom to the top of the oven.

Step #2: Position and drill holes in the side of the can to receive rod inserts, which create a rack inside the oven to support a pot. Use the same ¼-inch drill, if you wish. Locate the two grooves that run around the can—one about one-third the way up and one about two-thirds up. In each groove, position two pairs of holes opposite each other to allow you to slide a tent stake, skewer, or piece of bar stock through the can. Each pair should leave about 2½ inches of space between the rods. That gives a broad enough base to support whatever pan you choose when cooking in the oven.

By the way, if you don't have a drill, a church-key can opener will work for the vent holes. Just make sure you

Placing rod inserts for oven base.

don't punch a hole through the bottom of the oven. Otherwise you'll have open flames blasting into the vessel, searing your food into unrecognizable slag.

The pan used in this oven must be compact. My oven is 6 inches in diameter, and my pot, a small pint vessel from an old personal cook kit, is 5½ inches across. That allows for a ¼-inch space all the way around the pot when it's placed in the oven—sufficient for the convection currents to flow.

You don't have to use a pot. You could just wrap your food in foil and place it on the rack at either of the two levels available.

The two rack levels give you another way to control the cooking temperature in the oven. The lower rack position, closer to the heat source, is hotter; the upper one, cooler. You can also control the heat in the oven by raising or lowering the flame on the stove. Of course, there's no actual temperature reading here, unless you decide to bring along a meat thermometer. Trial and error is the rule with a one-pan homemade oven.

The top of the oven is any 6-inch diameter pot lid, or foil, or anything that keeps the heat in while allowing you to get at your meal every once in a while to test it for doneness.

The oven stows away just like your pot. You can nest the stove right inside along with other cooking items. When it's time to cook, everything comes out as a unit.

PACKING IT ALL AWAY

The great thing about one-pan cooking is that there's only so much equipment available to scatter around your campsite. You don't have two frying pans, two pots, and assorted lids clanking around underfoot. That one pan or oven does its job on top of the stove, or, once cooled and cleaned, quietly nestles away in a corner of your pack awaiting its next outing.

I'm not going through the science of packing a backpack here, except to briefly summarize what works for me:

1. Left side of the inside chamber is reserved for tent, clothing, and personal items
2. Right side features all the cooking gear stacked as follows from the bottom:
   - Pot and oven with stove nested, or
   - Stove with frying pan to one side
   - Cutting board laid in vertically along the narrow side of the pack
   - Kitchen kit, etc.
   - Fifty feet of rope and one small sack large enough to hold the food box—this is for the "bear bag" described in Chapter 3
3. Across the top, food stored in a Tupperware bread box

4. Water bottles are in the outside pockets or on my body; same for my big knife

That's about all there is to it. If you think about it, most of the kitchen you'll ever need or use is based on a commonsense approach to cookery. One-panning allows you to be more flexible in your choice of accessories and menus, the subject of the next chapter.

THE FOOD

We've talked about the setup for your trail feasts. Now let's look at how to plan your fun while still in the comfort of your living room.

HOW TO PLAN A MENU

If you're an active hiker or camper, you can require about 4,000 calories a day during the warmer months just to keep going. In the winter, you could use up to 6,000 calories a day between hiking and stamping your feet. Your body is an engine powered by the food (i.e., calories) you take in. Plan any meals you like, but build plenty of high-quality calories into them. And remember that these calories must be derived from the right sources.

I'm not a vegetarian. I like a balanced diet of meat and vegetable protein. But nothing about vegetarianism is incompatible with hiking. Chris Townsend, author of *The Backpacker's Handbook* (Ragged Mountain Press, 1993), is a vegetarian, and he's contributed a couple of his favorite recipes to this book. Chris's many 1,000-mile-plus hikes include the Continental Divide Trail from Mexico to Canada, and he's done them all on vegetables.

Whatever your preference, plan your meals to include, over the course of a day, ample quantities of the major food groups (see table).

I've always figured an average dinner serving after a day of active hiking to be about 4 to 6 ounces of meat, ¾ cup of vegetables (rehydrated if you're using dried peas, beans, etc.), about 2 to 3 ounces of bread or ½ cup of noo-

MAJOR FOOD GROUPS

Dairy Group

Milk, cheese, pudding, yogurt, tofu

Meat Group

Meats including beef, pork, poultry, fish, shellfish
Dried beans, peanut butter, eggs, nuts, seeds

Vegetable/Fruit Group

Berries, all fruits, all vegetables. Greens and leafy veggies
are excellent sources of roughage. Self-packaged and easy-
cooking choices include summer squash and green peppers.

Grain Group

Cereal, noodles, pastas, rice, grits, breads, popcorn

---

dles or rice, and a full piece of fruit (if fresh) or ½ cup of dried
fruits such as apricots, raisins, and prunes. The meat portion
is slightly elevated relative to an inactive diet, and the carbo-
hydrate intake is increased, yet fats are low. Your needs and
desires may vary. Nutritional substitutes are fine. The
accompanying table shows some of the alternatives to meat.

MEAT SUBSTITUTES

To obtain the equivalent level of protein found in one
ounce of meat, substitute as follows:

1 egg
¼ cup cashews, walnuts, almonds, pecans, or sun
    flower seeds
1½ cups cooked oatmeal
1 ounce cheese
2 tablespoons peanut butter
½ cup whole-wheat flour

To go farther—to ensure you get all nine amino acids
essential to your body's protein synthesis—practice protein
complementation. To show you how this works, the food
combinations listed below take advantage of protein complementation to provide complete protein. Each item on the

list contains all essential amino acids needed for protein synthesis.

Dairy Products or Eggs with Grains

Bread or rice pudding
Cereal and milk
Cheese fondue with bread
Cheese sandwich
Creamed soups with
    noodles or rice
Eggs and toast
Egg salad sandwich
Fettucine (pasta and cheese)

French toast
Macaroni and cheese
Meatless lasagna
Pancakes or waffles

Pizza
Quiche
Yogurt and crackers

Grains with Legumes

Baked beans and
    brown bread
Bean or lentil soup
    and bread
Bean and rice dishes
Corn tortillas or tacos
    and beans
Hummus (garbanzo
    bean paste) and bread

Lentils and rice

Peanut butter sandwich
Soybean sandwich

Split pea soup and cornbread

Tamale pie (beans and cornmeal)

Nuts and Seeds with Legumes

Bean soup with sesame seed muffins
Hummus with sesame seeds
Nuts and seed snacks
Roasted soybeans and seed snacks
Tofu with sesame seeds

Other Vegetables with Dairy Products or Eggs

Bean-cheese salad
Cream of vegetable soup
Eggplant-artichoke parmesan
Escalloped potatoes
Potato salad with egg
Spinach or broccoli quiche
Spinach salad with eggs and cheese

The bottom line is this: No one-pan menu is complete unless you obtain the nourishment you need to get up and keep going. Plan smart. Eat balanced meals.

You'll notice that most portions in this book are pretty large. At home the average size of the meat portion should be 3 to 4 ounces, but on the trail you'll need more. The suggested daily intake for an adult male is around 2,200 to 3,000 calories, but hiking demands a lot more fuel to keep your muscles chugging along. Depending on your weight, metabolism, and the load you're carrying, you could require upwards of 4,000 calories a day. Don't skimp on the food you pack.

And you never can tell, you might need an extra portion for a visitor. Or maybe that "Sunday morning out" turns into a "Sunday evening, I'm late thanks to the mud," and the extra meal comes in handy.

POWER BUYING

Since you'll be feeding yourself—the single most important guest at your outdoor table—don't cut corners on the quality of the food you purchase.

Fresh is always best, but there are times to use tinned meats, dried fruits and vegetables, or other prepared foods to facilitate your efforts. Just remember that whatever you carry in, you also have to carry out. That means cans, wrappers, foils, and the like. Avoid recipes that demand out-of-season vegetables or other exotic items.

As for meats, you might make friends with a good butcher. They tend to carry slightly better, though more expensive, cuts of meat, and you're better assured that the meat is fresh, not previously frozen.

Vegetables and fruits should always be ripe but firm. Even in the best of conditions, you'll be stressing them to the limit before they come near your pot. An extra day in a pack, even tucked closely to a frozen chuck of beef, can mean the difference between green beans almandine and squirrel food.

Powdered milk is an acceptable substitute for fresh when mixed in a ratio of 1 part powder to 3 parts water. Generally, though, I mix an entire packet of powder (designed to make 1 quart of milk) with 1 to 2 cups of water, depending on how thick I want the end result. It works fine in the recipes, and leftovers taste great in coffee. Unless you are depending on the milk fat for use in a sauce (evaporated milk may then be the only solution), powdered milk cooks well.

Cheese, however, is the greatest invention to make sure you get enough milk protein and fat. When on the trail, I can't get enough cheese. It keeps well and doesn't take up much space.

The "when" in shopping is just as important as the "what." Meats should be bought at least two days in advance to allow for freezing (see next section). Fruits and veggies can wait until the day before or, even better, the morning you leave. Most food stores restock throughout the day but tend to get their shipments early. The first fruits and vegetables on display most likely will be fresher than the ones that show up later in the day.

GETTING THE SHOW READY FOR THE ROAD

Creativity plays a big role when you're packing in a confined space. Repackaging, with a concentration on maintaining freshness and avoiding food poisoning, is a priority.

I use a Tupperware bread carrier as my primary food locker. It's big enough to hold 12,000 or so calories in the form of meat, eggs, veggies, drinks, sugars, and . . . well, enough food for three days for my small army of cells. This box (see photo) has a nice airtight top that seals in the food and seals out some of the nastiness that courses through a pack in a given day. It won't keep your food germ free—you have to do that—but it should keep the bugs and other critters out of it long enough for you to make a stew.

The box won't maintain temperature, but I've found a

The Tupperware breadbox, a backpack pantry.

way to keep meats (beef, poultry, pork) for 24 to 36 hours. First I plan my menus and determine what cuts of meat I'll need and in what weights. I then wrap each piece in heavy-duty, freezer-thickness aluminum foil and park the package in the deep freeze for two days. Then, about 10 minutes before I toss the pack into the trunk of my car, I pull the meat out of the freezer and wrap it in another layer of foil— loosely this time to leave some air space. Then into the box. There it will stay and keep, thawing as I go down the trail. It also helps keep other items in the box cool.

PACKAGING IDEAS

If you look for them, you'll find an incredible number of condiments packed in single-serving packets. Items such as soy sauce, ketchup, mustard, honey, and mayonnaise are packed in such a way as to require no refrigeration and little space. Find these (even if you have to raid your local fast-food emporium) and pack them away.

Other items demand more creative solutions. Oils can

be remeasured into vials, squeeze bottles, or even baby bottles. Flour, baking powder, pancake mix, and other dry ingredients can be measured into plastic bags and sealed. Remember to label these!

Vegetables come in their own wrappers. So does fruit. That's what makes fresh food so easy to handle.

Eggs require some cushioning to absorb shock, but the bigger problem is crushing them in a load shift. When I take eggs, I put them in either a small sealed food storage container or a special egg carrier.

Rice and pasta can be cooked at home and packaged in a plastic bag.

Again, most of this comes under the heading of common sense.

THE ONE-PAN MENU

Usually I'm on the trail for four meals, sometimes five. The four standard repasts are Saturday breakfast/lunch/dinner and Sunday breakfast. Sometimes I consider a late snack/dinner on Friday night. I'm pretty generous with myself when planning my food. I tend to overplan, ending up with a fuller belly than I might normally want. Then again, you never know when you might get stuck by weather in a high ridge shelter for an extra day. The additional food will be welcome.

Before we move on to a sample menu, I'd like to offer a lunch suggestion.

For a lot of trekkers, lunch is a brief break, just long enough to let muscles relax, feet cool, and maps be read. That might not leave enough time to cook a meal and clean up afterward. Here's a solution that tastes great and provides ample high-quality calories to keep you going until dinner. When I was an adult leader on a Boy Scout High Adventure in Minnesota, we kept a group of teenage boys going on an updated version of a historic backpacker fare. It was lunch for five of the nine days we were out. (My thanks to those fine folks who introduced me to this recipe and made our trip, and hundreds of others every year, enjoyable and memorable.)

Prepare this at home. Cut and wrap as many pieces as you want to carry.

HUDSON BAY BREAD

¾ cup (1½ sticks) butter or margarine
1 cup sugar
3 tablespoons Karo syrup
3 tablespoons honey
½ teaspoon maple flavoring

Cream the above ingredients. Mix together and add:

⅓ cup ground nuts (any combination)
4 cups oatmeal, uncooked

Spread mixture in two preheated 13 x 9 x 2-inch baking pans. (Press mixture down to a thickness of 1 to 1½ inches.) Bake at 325° F. for 25 minutes (check at about 20 minutes to prevent burning). When bread is done, remove from oven and immediately press down firmly with spatula. Cut into serving sizes (about the same as a slice of bread) while still warm. Makes 12 servings.

Serve this topped with peanut butter and jelly. You'll have a cold lunch that tastes great and is very filling. One slice should do it. You can substitute Hudson Bay Bread for any lunch you want.

Here's a sample of a typical trip menu that includes a cooked lunch and requires a frying pan.

Saturday Breakfast

Coffee
Sliced orange
Vegetable Eggs (see page 38)

Saturday Lunch

Juice mix
Parmy Shrooms n' Noodles (see page 58)
Pear, apple, or melon slice

Saturday Dinner
Sliced tomato
Hair-Raisin Curry Beef (see page 65)
Rice
Coconut Fruit Cup (see page 70)

Sunday Breakfast
Coffee
Juice mix
Ham slice
Apple Pancakes (see page 42)

You can also take along various snacks and hot drinks (coffee, hot chocolate, V-8 juice). The key is to get plenty of calories to keep up your energy, which, incidentally, preserves your body core temperature so you don't get chilled as easily.

CLEANUP

One of the big chores after any meal is washing the dishes and putting away the food. Roll up your sleeves. It's time to pay for your dinner.

There should be a small vial of chlorine bleach in the kitchen kit along with some dish soap. Here's where you put it to work.

First, scrape your cooking vessel clean of all food debris. (You might have done that already when you were digging for seconds or thirds.) But don't toss it, eat it! On the trail there's no garbage unless it's inedible, such as a banana peel. All of it is needed calories (read: fuel). Besides, dumping it in the woods attracts four-legged guests. Carry spoiled food out with you.

Now boil some water (carried from home or gathered and purified; remember, boiling and bleach may not affect *Giardia*) in your coffee pot. Pour some of the hot water into your cook pot. Add a few drops of dish soap and a little cold water. Scrub your cooking utensils first. Then the pot. Pour the soapy water out in the woods, at least

100 feet from any stream or pond.

Using a little more of your hot water, rinse your pot and utensils clean of any remaining soapy residue. You might want to grip the pan with your hot-pot tongs to keep from burning your hand. Dump the water in the woods as before.

Now add the balance of your hot water to the pot, making sure your utensils are inside. Add a few drops of bleach to kill any germs. Swish the water over all parts of the pot and utensils. Dump it as before. Air dry all. Pack away when finished.

A CLEAN SITE IS A HAPPY SITE

The view of your site should be just as pleasant as the view you have when you look away from your camp. After dinner take a few moments to pick up your gear, putting what you don't need for the night back in your pack. The last thing you want to leave out is food. Especially in your tent!

Almost any place worth camping in comes equipped with a full complement of night-foraging critters. Most are small, like raccoons, but they can still rip a pretty big hole in a pack. Some, however, are the size of a small car, and are capable of sniffing out tasty morsels even if they are in a tent next to a smelly human. If you don't want a bear trashing your tent or your gear, get your food up and out of the way.

This is where rigging a bear bag comes in handy. With 50 feet of line, you can keep your food box in one piece for breakfast.

Locate two trees about 20 to 25 feet apart. Throw one end of the line over a branch about 12 to 14 feet off the ground on one tree (tying a rock to the end if necessary). Tie off the end. At the other tree, throw the other end of the line over a branch about the same height off the ground, allowing the line between the trees to sag to the ground for the moment. Tie the food bag to the line midway between the trees, then take up on the second end to remove the sag from the line and hoist the food bag as high as possible off the ground. Tie off the end.

   That's the simplest method to describe, but there are

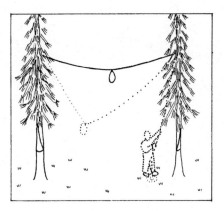

Line is placed over branches
before attaching food bag.

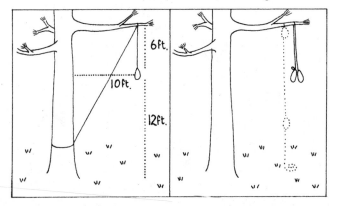

Food bag may be hung   Counterbalance system:
from long strong branch.   retrieve using a stick.

The bear bag.

any number of variations. Remember to put everything aromatic in the bear bag, including food, suntan lotion, and tobacco.

A quick comment. Some outdoors cookbook authors suggest chilling food in streams overnight. It's a neat idea, if there isn't any wildlife around. But my oddsmaker says the chances are pretty good that a varmint will eat your pudding well before you do.

THE FRYING PAN

So far we've talked about the various pots, pans, kettles, ovens, and other paraphernalia you can lug along to make sure you're well fed on the trail. In this chapter, we'll get down to the brass tacks of eating.

BREAKFAST

Most of us remember the smell of thick-cut bacon sizzling in a pan and the aroma of fresh-brewed coffee in almost instinctive fashion. Breakfast is the most important meal on the trail, as far as I'm concerned. It's what gives you the old get-up-and-go. So eat hearty and walk on!

Eggs

Scrambled eggs are probably the most basic form of trail eggs going. It means never having to say you're sorry for broken yolks. You can spruce up scrambled eggs in any number of ways, with additions of meat, cheese, and/or spices. Here's how I make mine.

SPRUCED-UP SCRAMBLED EGGS

2 or 3 large eggs
3 tablespoons milk (or powdered milk and water in 1:3 ratio)
salt and pepper to taste
1 tablespoon vegetable oil
extras (see list below)

Beat eggs, milk, and salt and pepper in a bowl. Preheat frying pan and add oil. Pour eggs into pan and let cook undisturbed for about 30 seconds. Add the desired extra ingredients (see below) and mix in with spatula, scraping bottom of pan as you continue to turn the eggs until dry (or as done as you like). Eat with a hard roll, fruit, and beverage.

SCRAMBLED EGGS EXTRAS

Meat	Cheese
Diced ham or steak	Any block cheese, diced
Sliced hot dog	Cream cheese, cubed
Shredded baloney	**Spices**
Sliced salami	Tabasco sauce
Chicken chunks	Oregano, basil

If you're an egg fanatic, there are ways to make the dependable, edible egg more exciting: Add dried mushrooms, parsley, onions, or green peppers. Or put crunch into your meal with walnuts, cashews, or peanuts. And if you're really adventurous, try adding dried fruits, such as apricots, along with nuts.

Sometimes you have to make an even bigger meal out of breakfast. Spicing things up while getting something a bit more substantial into your stomach can make a dark and damp morning bright indeed.

VEGETABLE EGGS

1 tablespoon vegetable oil
2 medium potatoes (¾ cup or so), chopped
¼ cup green pepper, chopped
1 small onion, chopped
salt and pepper to taste
2 eggs
¼ cup diced cheese (cheddar, Monterey Jack, or prefer-
    ence, optional)
1 tablespoon bread crumbs (optional)

Heat frying pan over medium heat. Add oil and sauté vegetables until browned, but not crisp. Add salt and pepper to taste. Break eggs over vegetable mixture and cover. Lower heat and cook until eggs are to your liking. Sprinkle with cheese and bread crumbs, if desired.

And if you want to be a bit more ethnic with your eggs, consider these three egg dishes. You'll think you're walking around the Mediterranean when you taste them.

EGGS À LA HAIFA

¼ lb kosher salami, sliced
1 teaspoon olive oil
3 eggs
salt and pepper to taste
1 teaspoon peanut oil

Notch edges of salami slices so they won't curl while cooking. Preheat frying pan, add olive oil, and cook salami slowly. Turn once so that each side is crispy. Drain off oil. In small bowl, beat eggs and season as desired with salt and pepper. Add peanut oil to pan. Return salami slices to pan and add eggs. Fry slowly, as for an omelette, until bottom is golden brown and top is firm. Slide out of pan onto plate and flip back into pan to brown top. Watch carefully so as not to burn.

FLOR-EGG-ENZO

1½ tablespoons olive oil
½ small onion, diced
a pinch of salt
⅛ teaspoon pepper
1 tomato, chopped
½ cup dried peas, rehydrated
¼ cup water
2 eggs
1½ tablespoons Parmesan cheese
chunks of French or Italian bread (optional)

Preheat frying pan and add oil. Sauté onions until tender. Lower heat and add salt (if desired), pepper, and tomatoes. Simmer for about 20 minutes. Add peas and water and simmer another 10 minutes. Carefully break eggs into mixture in pan as you would for poached eggs. Continue cooking over low heat for another 20 minutes without stirring. Sprinkle with Parmesan. If desired, gently add the chunks of bread to mixture about 10 minutes before serving to soak up a bit of sauce and thicken things.

HUEVOS AND TACOS

2 or 3 flour tortillas
3 eggs
2 oz muenster cheese, chopped or shredded
dash Tabasco sauce
1 avocado, diced
1 tablespoon black olives, diced
1 teaspoon vegetable oil
salsa (optional)

Warm tortillas in dry frying pan; set aside in covered dish to keep warm. In a bowl, mix eggs, cheese, and hot sauce. Add oil to hot frying pan and scramble egg mixture. When done, remove from heat and stir in avocado and olives. Spoon onto warm tortillas, roll, and top with salsa (if desired).

Omelettes

I guess you could say that omelettes are scrambled eggs that have a sense of togetherness. You can customize your omelette any way you wish, but if you don't cook it right from the start, you might as well make scrambled eggs.

DON'S BASIC OMELETTE

2 or 3 large eggs
1 tablespoon water
1 teaspoon peanut oil

Gently beat eggs to break yolks, but don't blend completely. Add water and beat until froth begins to build. Preheat pan and add oil. Pour eggs into pan slowly, allowing eggs to spread evenly across bottom of pan. Rotate pan gently to build a lip around edge. Cook slowly until top is firm and bottom is lightly browned. Add desired extras (meat, cheese, veggie, or whatever) to half of omelette. Loosen omelette from pan by gently sliding spatula underneath. Slowly slide omelette half out of pan onto plate; flip remaining half over to close omelette. Heat of egg will melt cheese and heat veggies and meat.

OMELETTE À LA TERRY RODRIGUEZ

1 tablespoon each olive oil, vegetable oil
½ medium potato, sliced (leave skin on)
½ medium onion, chopped
2 or 3 eggs
small handful pimento-stuffed olives, sliced
pepper to taste

Heat frying pan. Heat oils in pan and cook potatoes and onion until tender. Remove from pan with slotted spoon. Beat eggs and olives together with pepper. Pour in pan and cook over low heat until partially cooked. Slide spatula around the edges periodically to loosen from pan. Add onion and potato and fold omelette. Cook until firm.

You can, of course, cook your eggs in a variety of ways, from frying to poaching. If you can't figure out fried eggs by now, well . . .

Did you know you can poach eggs in a frying pan? Serve them on toast over a slice of ham and cheese, if you like.

POACHED EGGS

1 cup water
2 or 3 eggs
1 teaspoon vinegar (cider, wine, or white)

Boil water in frying pan. Add vinegar and gently break eggs into lightly rolling water. As eggs solidify, roll them with a serving spoon to keep tendrils from spreading. When cooked to taste (I like about 4 to 5 minutes), remove from pan with slotted spoon.

Then again, eggs of another sort can include the easiest way I know to combine scrambled eggs and maple syrup.

FRENCH TOAST

2 or 3 slices bread, slightly stale
2 or 3 eggs
1 teaspoon vegetable oil
maple syrup, jelly, or powdered sugar (optional)

Preheat frying pan. In a bowl, beat eggs. Dip bread slices (you can make them stale just by leaving them out in air for about a half hour) and soak in egg mixture until thoroughly moist. Add oil to pan and place in one or two slices (depending on size of pan) to cook. Allow to brown well before flipping. Remove to plate and serve with favorite topping.

Cakes—Griddle, Pan, and Otherwise

Sometimes eggs just aren't what you want. You want the old-fashioned trail breakfast, the one that'll stick to your ribs all day long. Pioneers called them johnnycakes. Whatever you name them, they're fun and sooo good.

PANCAKES IN A SACK

Mix these ingredients at home and place in bag:
1 cup all-purpose flour
1 teaspoon white or yellow cornmeal
1 teaspoon brown sugar
¾ teaspoon salt
¾ teaspoon baking soda
1 teaspoon baking powder

At campsite add the following:
1 egg
1 cup milk

Mix all ingredients together in bowl until blended but still lumpy. Preheat frying pan and rub a bit of vegetable oil into pan. Fry until golden brown; flip and cook other side. Serve with maple syrup and bacon or sausage.

You can also take the basic pancake recipe and add blueberries, bananas, or other fruit. And then there are some really ambitious ways to present the basic pancake.

APPLE PANCAKES

2 apples, cored, peeled, and chopped
¼ cup maple syrup
2 tablespoons margarine
1 cup milk (or powdered milk with equivalent water)
1 egg
½ tablespoon liquefied Crisco shortening
¾ cup Bisquick
¼ teaspoon cinnamon
¼ teaspoon nutmeg

Combine apple, syrup, and 1 tablespoon oil in hot frying pan and cook until tender. Mix milk, egg, ½ tablespoon oil, baking mix, cinnamon, and nutmeg to make batter. Remove apples from frying pan (reserve liquid) and add to batter. Spoon batter into hot frying pan. When dry bubbles appear, turn once and cook until golden brown. Serve with reserved liquid from apples.

LUNCH AND DINNER

You can load up on food whenever you like in whatever level of complication you wish. We'll just divide things up by protein source starting with fowl things.

Poultry

You can substitute any type of bird in recipes calling for chicken as far as I'm concerned—duck, pheasant, game hen, or turkey. Just enjoy its low-fat nature.

I suggest you buy your chicken fresh. Since most stores don't package poultry in convenient single-serving sizes, you will have to repackage before your trip. The problem is that much of the chicken you find on the meat counter has been frozen at least once (if it is not frozen when you buy it). To thaw, repackage, and refreeze is a real no-no, because the moment meat is thawed, germs start to grow, and they continue to grow until the meat is refrozen completely. While the chicken is thawing in your pack, the germs can flourish again. Your meal could be spoiled before you get the chance to cook it, and your stomach could be, too, if you cook and eat spoiled meat.

Given good-quality meat, poultry can make for some very interesting and satisfying trail meals.

WALNUT CHICKEN

¼ cup vegetable oil
1 cup walnuts
1 tablespoon cornstarch
2 tablespoons cold water
2 tablespoons soy sauce
2 chicken breasts, boned
1 chicken bouillon cube
¾ cup boiling water
1 teaspoon salt (optional)
1 cup rice, precooked

Note: Chicken breasts as commonly presented at the meat counter are really one breast cut in half and laid open to look something like a Valentine heart; count this arrangement as two. Heat oil in frying pan over high heat. Fry walnuts lightly (do not brown). Remove walnuts and reserve oil. Mix cornstarch, cold water, and soy sauce with 3 tablespoons of reserved oil. Pour into hot pan; add chicken and brown. Dissolve bouillon cube in boiling water; add to pan. Stir in salt (if desired) and walnuts. Stir until thick and serve over precooked rice. You could add slices of green pepper after browning chicken, if you like.

If you like a somewhat Oriental theme (you can even use a wok), there are a lot of different chicken dishes that will spice up your dinner.

PODS 'N BIRDS

2 chicken breasts, boned and cut in 1" pieces (see note
    in Walnut Chicken recipe above)
¼ cup cornstarch
1 egg white
2 tablespoons white wine
2 tablespoons peanut oil
4 mushrooms, sliced
¼ lb fresh snow peas
¼ teaspoon salt (optional)

¼ teaspoon ginger
¼ cup nuts (any kind)
¼ cup watercress (optional)
1 cup rice, precooked

Dredge chicken in cornstarch. Combine egg white and wine, first separating white from yolk by carefully breaking egg in half and passing yolk and white from shell to shell until yolk is in one shell and most of the white is in the other. Beat well and set aside. Heat 1 tablespoon of oil in frying pan until it smokes. Sauté mushrooms, snow peas, ginger, and salt (if desired) for 2 minutes. Remove from pan with slotted spoon. Add remaining oil to pan. Add chicken to egg-white mixture in bowl. Add to pan and sauté for about 2 minutes. Add nuts and any additional vegetables you like, such as watercress, and cook about 3 to 4 more minutes. Serve with rice.

DELHI CHICKEN WITH RICE

1 tablespoon vegetable oil
1 medium onion, chopped
2 chicken breasts, boned and cut in 1" cubes (see note in Walnut Chicken recipe, page 44)
1 tablespoon flour
¼ teaspoon ginger
1 to 2 tablespoons curry powder (or to taste)
2 tablespoons honey
2 tablespoons soy sauce
2 chicken bouillon cubes
2 cups water
¾ cup white rice, raw
1 or 2 carrots, sliced

Heat oil in pan. Add onion and sauté until brown. Add chicken and brown. Sprinkle flour, ginger, and curry powder into pan and stir. Add honey, soy sauce, bouillon cubes, and water. Simmer for 5 minutes. Add rice and carrots. Stir and simmer uncovered for another 20 to 25 minutes.

The following is a variation on Delhi Chicken with Rice that presents a little different flavor.

BOMBAY BREAST

  2 chicken breasts, boned and cut in 1" cubes (see note
      in Walnut Chicken recipe, page 44)
  ¼ cup soy sauce
  2 tablespoons lime juice
  1 tablespoon honey
  ¼ teaspoon curry powder
  1 green pepper, chopped
  1 red pepper, chopped
  ½ cup bean sprouts
  1 tablespoon peanut oil

In a bowl, mix all ingredients except oil. Marinate for 20 minutes. Heat pan over high flame until very hot (to test, drip a bead of water into pan; it should dance). Drain marinade. Stir-fry in pan for about 5 minutes or until veggies are tender. If you wish to use the marinade as a sauce, you must bring it to a boil in the fry pan after the meat and vegetables are removed.

Then again, maybe your taste is more Mediterranean than Bengali.

CHICKEN SCALLOPINE

  2 chicken breasts, boned and cut in 1" cubes (see note
      in Walnut Chicken recipe, page 44)
  ¼ cup flour
  salt and pepper to taste
  1 egg
  1 to 2 tablespoons olive oil
  1 clove garlic, peeled and sliced
  1 chicken bouillon cube
  ¾ cup boiling water
  ¼ cup dry red wine
  4 mushrooms, sliced
  1 to 1½ cups precooked spaghetti or pasta

Place flour, salt, and pepper in plastic bag. In a bowl, beat the egg. Dip chicken into egg and then place in bag with flour. Shake until well coated. Heat oil in pan and sauté garlic until it begins to brown. Lower heat, add chicken, and sauté slowly until brown. Add bouillon cube, water, wine, and mushrooms. Simmer uncovered for 15 minutes. Add pasta and heat through.

Note: You can substitute veal cutlets for the chicken.

CHICKEN CATCH-A-TORY

½ lb boned chicken (white or dark pieces)
salt and pepper to taste
garlic powder to taste
2 tablespoons olive oil
1 medium onion, sliced
1 medium green pepper, sliced
1 6-oz can tomato paste
1 cup water
4 to 6 mushrooms, sliced
¼ teaspoon oregano

Coat chicken with salt, pepper, and garlic powder. Heat oil in pan; add chicken and brown. Remove chicken. Add onion and green pepper to pan and sauté until tender. Add tomato paste, water, mushrooms, oregano, and chicken. Cover and cook for 30 minutes over medium flame.

This recipe goes well with rice, rice cakes, or bread.

HONG KONG BIRD, OR CHICKEN CRUNCH

½ lb boned chicken (white or dark pieces)
2 tablespoons peanut oil
½ cup orange juice
½ teaspoon ginger
½ cup raisins
1 6-oz can water chestnuts, sliced
½ cup white wine
½ cup salted cashews
1 tablespoon cornstarch and 2 tablespoons water

Heat oil in pan. Add chicken and brown. Reduce heat and add all ingredients except cashews and cornstarch. Simmer for 30 minutes. Add cashews. Using whisk, mix cornstarch and water in cup and add as needed to thicken sauce.

How many peanut butter sandwiches have you faced? And how many times have you stared at that jar and wondered if there was something else you could do with it? Here's one for you. It can be served with granola or other grain.

STICKY CHICKEN

2 chicken breasts, boned and cut in 1" cubes (see note
     in Walnut Chicken recipe, page 44)
¼ cup peanut butter
1 tablespoon honey
2 tablespoons soy sauce
⅛ teaspoon garlic powder
1 tablespoon lemon juice
¼ teaspoon cayenne pepper
2 medium onions, chopped
1 cup water
1 tablespoon ketchup
salt and pepper to taste

Combine all ingredients in pan and cook over medium flame until chicken is cooked.

You'll notice that I tend to specify boned chicken. It really doesn't make any difference, but this way you don't have to carry out the chicken bones when you're done eating. Those small bones and splinters can tear the living daylights out of some poor scavenger's gullet if you dump them in the woods.

Once in a while, I pack some butter instead of oils. It's great for its milk fat content, as in the following sauce.

SAUCY CHICKEN

White Sauce
2 tablespoons butter
2 tablespoons flour
1 cup milk (or powdered milk and water in 1:3 ratio)

In pan, melt butter over low heat. Blend in flour and gradually add milk and cook, stirring constantly, for 5 minutes until sauce is smooth. Set aside in cup, clean pan, and continue with the following.

2 chicken breasts, boned (see note in Walnut Chicken recipe, page 44)
1 teaspoon salt
¼ teaspoon white pepper
¼ cup (½ stick) butter
½ cup dry white wine
¾ cup white sauce
1 medium green pepper, cut in strips

Rub chicken with salt and pepper. In preheated pan over medium flame, melt half the butter and lightly brown chicken. Add wine and white sauce. Cook 20 minutes. Add remaining butter and green pepper. Cook until hot, but do not burn sauce. Can be served with precooked rice or noodles.

But just maybe your taste is for something a little redder.

CHICKEN PAPRI-CRASH

½ lb boned chicken (white or dark pieces)
salt and pepper to taste
garlic powder to taste
2 tablespoons peanut oil
1 medium onion, sliced thin
1 medium green pepper, cut in strips
1 medium tomato, chopped
2 chicken bouillon cubes
1 cup water
1 tablespoon paprika (Hungarian is best)
½ cup Minute Rice

Rub chicken with salt, pepper, and garlic powder. To preheated pan, add oil and chicken. Brown chicken on both sides. Add onion and green pepper and cook for 2 or 3 minutes. Add tomato, bouillon cubes, and water. Bring to boil. Add paprika and stir. Cover and cook for 10 minutes over medium heat. Five minutes before serving, add Minute Rice to simmering sauce. Cook for 1 minute and let stand 4 minutes, covered (make sure all rice is soaking in sauce, or you'll find some unexpected crunch).

Apples are one of the easiest fruits to pack. They come with their own packaging and are 100 percent biodegradable.

HENS 'N APPLE

1 Cornish hen, quartered
2 tablespoons vegetable oil
½ teaspoon garlic powder
1 small onion, chopped
salt and pepper to taste
¼ cup dry white wine
1 medium apple (MacIntosh, Granny Smith, or other
     sharpish apple), chopped

Preheat pan, add oil, and brown hen. Sprinkle with salt, pepper, and garlic powder and add onion. Add wine and cover. Simmer for 10 minutes. Stir in apple and cover again. Cook another 10 minutes or until apples are quite soft. You can add a few small white potatoes with the wine for added carbohydrates.

Going back to butter as a substitute for oils, here's something we're all familiar with.

CHICKEN À LA KING
4 tablespoons water
1 chicken breast, boned and diced
2 tablespoons margarine
2 tablespoons flour
1 cup milk (make from powdered)
¼ teaspoon salt (optional)
pepper to taste
1 small green pepper, chopped
3 mushrooms, sliced
1 egg yolk, slightly beaten

In preheated pan, heat water to rolling boil. Place chicken in water to poach. Stir meat constantly to avoid sticking. When tender (no more than 4 or 5 minutes), remove chicken and dispose of water. Return pan to flame and melt margarine. Sauté green pepper and mushrooms. Sprinkle veggies with flour and stir. Add milk and seasonings. Cook until thick, stirring constantly. Add chicken and egg yolk. Cook another 10 minutes over medium heat, stirring to keep from scorching. Serve over bread, biscuits, or other grain.

BASIL WRATHBONED CHICKEN

2 chicken breasts, boned (see note in Walnut Chicken
    recipe, page 44)
¼ cup flour
salt and pepper
¼ cup olive oil
1 tablespoon green onion, chopped
½ cup sliced green beans
1 chicken bouillon cube
½ cup water
1 large tomato, chopped
½ teaspoon basil
1 tablespoon vegetable oil
1 cup precooked pasta
Parmesan cheese (optional)

Combine flour, salt, and pepper in bowl. Dredge
chicken in flour mixture. Preheat pan and add half the oil.
Add chicken and cook until tender. Discard oil. Add
remaining oil to pan. Sauté onions and beans for 1 to 2
minutes. Add bouillon cube, water, tomato, and basil.
Simmer uncovered for 5 minutes. Remove from pan. Add
last tablespoon oil and precooked pasta to pan to reheat
it. Serve chicken over pasta and sprinkle with Parmesan.

There are probably a thousand ways to clog your arter-
ies with fried chicken. Let's do it simple and then have
some fun. Just be careful not to try the next few recipes in
the rain. Water in hot oil spatters furiously and can easily
burn you. For that matter, be careful with hot oil even
when it's not raining. Hot oil can cause some of the nasti-
est burns an outdoorsperson will ever face.

SQUARE-ONE FRIED CHICKEN

1 egg
½ cup milk
salt and pepper to taste
½ cup flour
½ lb chicken (white or dark pieces)
4 to 5 tablespoons vegetable oil

Beat together egg, milk, salt, and pepper. Roll chicken in flour, then in egg mixture, then in flour again. Preheat pan and heat oil until it bubbles. Be very careful! Brown chicken on all sides. Cover and cook over low flame for 20 minutes or until chicken is cooked through. Remove chicken to plate and blot with paper towel to absorb excess oil.

CHICKEN GONE CRACKERS

Same as the above formula but substitute ¼ cup crushed saltine crackers and ¼ cup white cornmeal for the flour. Add about ¼ teaspoon of garlic powder to egg mixture. Cook as suggested in Square-One recipe.

LUIGI'S FRIED CHICKEN

This time you keep the flour but add ¼ teaspoon garlic powder to the egg mixture and ½ teaspoon oregano to the flour. Also, you cook in olive oil. You can add some basil to the flour, as well.

BATTER-UP FRIED CHICKEN

Combine egg mixture and flour together to make a batter. Add flour as needed to thicken so you get an even, deep coating on your bird. You'll also want extra oil; maybe increase it to ⅓ to ½ cup. Cook uncovered.

MR. NATURAL'S FRIED FOWL

2 eggs
½ cup milk
¼ cup flour
½ cup granola, oatmeal, or other grain
salt and pepper to taste
½ lb chicken (white or dark pieces)
½ cup peanut oil

Mix eggs, milk, flour, and grain together to form a batter. If batter seems thin, add more flour. Rub salt and pepper on the chicken and then dip it in the batter. Preheat pan and add oil. When oil bubbles, place chicken in pan and cook thoroughly, turning periodically until tender. Remove chicken to paper towel.

CHEESY FRIED CHICKEN

1 egg
¼ cup milk
¼ teaspoon salt (optional)
¼ teaspoon pepper
1 tablespoon Parmesan cheese
½ lb chicken (white or dark pieces)
½ cup flour
2 tablespoons butter or margarine
3 to 4 tablespoons olive oil
3 tablespoons lemon juice
2 teaspoons whole pine nuts
1 teaspoon fresh parsley, chopped

Beat egg, milk, salt, pepper, and cheese. Dredge chicken in flour, dip it in egg mixture, and dredge it in flour again. Preheat pan and add butter and oil; heat until bubbling. Add chicken and brown on all sides. Lower heat and cook until chicken is tender (maybe 20 minutes). Remove chicken. To remaining oil in pan, add lemon juice, pine nuts, and parsley. Cook for 1 minute or until nuts are browned. Pour over chicken.

Here's a foreign food that's fun to make, fun to eat, and, I think, good for you. You can cook veggies, beef, or poultry this way. I favor a mix.

TEMPURA BATTER

1 egg
¼ teaspoon salt (optional)
¼ teaspoon sugar
½ cup cold water
⅓ cup flour

Beat eggs, salt, and sugar in bowl until frothy. Continue beating while adding cold water. Add flour and mix well, but don't overdo it. The batter holds best if you can keep it cold, say by placing it in another bowl of chilled water .

You'll need a lot of oil. Depending on the size of your frying pan, you might need as little as ½ cup peanut oil to as much as 2 cups. The rule is, you need enough oil so that whatever you fry in it floats. Then heat the oil until it bubbles.

You can cook any vegetable—from potatoes to squash, from broccoli to carrots—and any meat in this batter. Just make sure that your pieces (especially for solid veggies like carrots) are not too thick to fry. I'd suggest:

CHICKEN TEMPURA

1 chicken breast, boned and cut in strips
1 or 2 carrots, peeled and sliced
1 green pepper, cut in strips
1 small Vidalia (sweet) onion, sliced 1/8" thick
1 cup rice, precooked (optional)

Dip everything into the batter a few pieces at a time and add to hot oil. Cook until lightly browned. Remove to a paper towel to drain. Remove crumbs from oil with slotted spoon before adding next batch. Serve alone or with rice. Soy sauce is a nice touch.

Vegetables

There are a lot of folks who like to take a day off every
once in a while from eating meat. Maybe a main dish that
centers around something green. It's a nice change of pace
and eliminates the need (usually) for radical refrigeration.
Just remember that vegetables bruise easily and, when
dinged, spoil fast.

EGGPLANT RAGOUT

1 small eggplant, sliced Julienne style
1 medium tomato, chopped
1 small onion, chopped
1 small green pepper, chopped
1 6-oz can tomato paste
½ cup water
salt and pepper to taste
¼ teaspoon paprika
¼ teaspoon basil
Parmesan cheese (optional)

Put everything in a large frying pan. Stir and simmer
until veggies are soft and sauce is thick (about 30 minutes). You might also add some Parmesan cheese to
thicken the base.

Many times the veggie role in a meal in the wild is as a
side dish. Remember that you can usually cook any vegetables you want in the side of your frying pan—accepting
the fact that you may, from time to time, have to live with
a bit of unusual sauce as a complement to your greens.

ROAD HOUSE HASHBROWNS

1 tablespoon peanut oil
1 medium onion, chopped
1 large potato, sliced thin (leave peel on)
salt and pepper to taste
leftover bacon, salami, or other meat, diced (optional)

Heat pan over medium flame and add oil. Sauté onions in oil until tender, but not crisp. Add all other ingredients and continue cooking until potatoes begin to stick to pan. This goes well with red meats, but fits any meal. A real belly warmer.

MOUNTAIN FRIES

2 large potatoes, cut in ¼" spears (leave skin on)
¼ cup vegetable oil
1 tablespoon Tabasco sauce
seasoned salt (optional)

Place potatoes and Tabasco sauce in plastic bag and shake to coat. Heat oil in pan. Add potatoes and cook for 3 to 5 minutes, stirring occasionally to prevent sticking. Remove with slotted spoon. Drain on cloth or paper towel. Sprinkle with seasoned salt. My kind of hot!

SPUDS 'N PEPPERS

1 jalapeño pepper, diced (watch it, these are potent)
1 to 2 tablespoons oil or margarine
1 small green pepper, sliced thin
1 small red pepper, sliced thin
2 medium potatoes, peeled and sliced thin
salt and pepper to taste
garlic powder to taste

First you have to roast the jalapeño pepper: Devise a type of rack in the frying pan—maybe a piece of aluminum foil—to keep the jalapeño off surface of pan. Place jalapeño on rack, cover and roast for 5 to 10 minutes over high flame. Remove pepper from pan and peel it. Place oil in pan and heat. Add all vegetables and fry until browned and crispy. Add seasonings as desired.

To make a complete meal of this, push the vegetables to side of the pan and cook a boneless breast of chicken in the juices for about 10 minutes, flipping occasionally.

PARMY SHROOMS 'N NOODLES

   1 tablespoon peanut oil
   3 mushrooms, diced
   1 small onion, diced
   ½ cup milk
   1 cup noodles, precooked
   ½ cup ham, diced (optional)
   ¼ cup Parmesan cheese

   Heat frying pan over medium heat. Add oil and sauté vegetables until tender, but not brown. Drain oil. Add milk, noodles, ham, and cheese and toss over low heat for a minute or two until mixture is hot.

SUNSHINE SQUASH

   2 tablespoons peanut oil
   1 medium onion, diced
   1 medium summer squash, diced
   5 to 6 mushrooms, sliced or chopped
   ¼ to ½ teaspoon garlic powder
   ¼ teaspoon pepper
   salt to taste

   Preheat frying pan over medium flame. Add oil and sauté onion until tender. Add squash and cook uncovered until desired tenderness (I like mine "crisp-tender"). Add the mushrooms and seasonings and cook for about 3 to 4 more minutes.

   Blanching vegetables at home is an easy way to make sure you have cooked vegetables on the trail. Usually, blanching works best with firm green vegetables such as beans, broccoli, zucchini, and pea pods. But you can shorten your cooking time with any fry-pan vegetable by taking a few minutes at home to blanche them and then repack them in a bag. Boil about 2 cups water (salt optional) in a pot. Place the desired vegetables in water and cook for 2 minutes—no more, no less. Drain immediately. Let cool and place in plastic bag. Here's a tasty way to use those home-blanched green beans.

MCAULIFFE'S GREEN BEANS

1 tablespoon vegetable oil
¾ cup green beans, sliced
2 oz almonds, sliced

Heat frying pan over low flame. Add oil and let heat. Add almonds and fry them gently (be careful not to burn them). Add beans and increase heat to medium flame. Toss beans and almonds together for about 1 minute—long enough for veggies to heat, but not long enough for almonds to burn.

STIR FRY VEGETABLES

3 tablespoons peanut oil
1½ cups mixed vegetables (green beans, pea pods, diced carrots, diced onions, mushrooms, green or red peppers)
1 tablespoon soy sauce
salt and pepper to taste

Heat frying pan over high flame (drop of water on surface should jump). Add oil and let heat. Add vegetables and stir fry for about 2 to 3 minutes. Add soy sauce, salt, and pepper. Toss and stir-fry for another minute. Pour over precooked rice or serve with bread.

POTATO PANCAKES

2 potatoes, peeled and grated
1 egg, beaten
1 tablespoon flour
½ teaspoon baking powder
1 tablespoon butter or margarine

Combine all ingredients except butter and form into flat cakes. Over medium flame, heat butter. Cook like regular pancakes, turning to brown both sides.

Meat

Yes, you can substitute bear and venison for beef, if you wish. But whatever meat you do use, make sure that it's high quality and well trimmed to eliminate waste (bones, gristle, and fat).

Although most of the following recipes specify particular cuts, you can usually substitute any grade. In recipes calling for hamburger or ground beef, I like to use 85 percent lean or leaner. If all else fails, go with chopped, ground, sliced, or whole top sirloin. It's lean and usually tender enough for most combinations.

Often, though, you'll start out cooking with hamburger. It's forgiving of beginners and weary hikers.

HAMBURGER HASH

½ lb ground beef
½ medium onion, diced
¼ cup pinto beans (previously soaked and packed in plastic bag)
2 oz ketchup
1 tablespoon brown sugar
½ cup water
1 beef bouillon cube
salt and pepper to taste

Brown beef and add onion. Cook until tender. Add all remaining ingredients. Stir mixture and simmer for 10 to 15 minutes or until sauce is smooth.

PURPLE BURGER

½ lb ground beef
1 small onion, minced
¼ cup pickled beets, diced
½ cup cooked potato, diced
¼ teaspoon salt (optional)
⅛ teaspoon black pepper
1 tablespoon margarine

In bowl, gently mix all ingredients except margarine. Heat frying pan over medium flame. Melt margarine in pan and spoon mixture onto hot surface. Flatten with spatula to about 1 inch. Cover and cook for 3 to 5 minutes or until browned. Flip once, cover, and finish cooking for another 5 minutes or until done. Serve with hardtack or rye bread.

What hike would be complete without at least one dose of something to warm the insides and stretch the limits of your compatriot's patience?

CHILI BLAST

1 lb stew beef or steak, cut into ½" cubes
1 small onion, chopped
1 clove garlic, minced
2 tablespoons vegetable oil
½ cup dried corn, rehydrated
1 6-oz can tomato paste
1¼ cups water
2 chili peppers (mild or hot), seeded and chopped
¼ teaspoon salt (optional)
spices to taste (cumin, coriander, or chili powder)
one or more of following (optional): raisins, grapes, summer squash, zucchini, cactus ears

In frying pan, cook onion, beef, and garlic in oil until beef is browned. Add all other ingredients except optional ones. Bring to boil and reduce heat. Simmer covered for about 30 minutes. Add desired optional ingredients and simmer for about 10 more minutes or until meat is tender.

Sometimes you might want to make a round meal rather than a square one in your frying pan. And what better way to celebrate nature than with meatballs accompanied by hash browns? Or stir-fried green beans? Or raw sliced zucchini?

SOUPY MEATBALLS

½ lb ground beef
¼ cup seasoned bread crumbs
½ medium onion, diced
salt and pepper to taste
2 tablespoons corn oil
1 cup water
1 packet beef-based soup mix (single-serving size)

Combine meat, bread crumbs, onion, and salt and pepper. Shape into meatballs about 1 to 1½ inches in diameter. Heat frying pan and add oil. Brown meatballs. Roll them around to brown. Add water and soup mix. Simmer for 5 to 10 minutes. If desired, add thinly sliced potato (unpeeled) or other veggies to bubbling mix.

SWEDISH MEATBALLS

½ lb ground sirloin
¼ teaspoon sugar
1 egg
¼ teaspoon sage
¼ teaspoon allspice
¼ teaspoon nutmeg
1 small onion, finely chopped
1 cup bread crumbs
⅓ cup cold water
1 tablespoon vegetable oil

Mix all ingredients (except oil) together in bowl and knead well. Shape into 1-inch meatballs. Heat oil in frying pan and brown over medium flame. Roll meatballs around until cooked through. Cover and simmer for about 20 minutes, periodically rolling meatballs. If you like, you can add sliced potato and onion before simmering.

GYPSY MEATBALLS

Same as above, but substitute uncooked Minute Rice for bread crumbs, and oregano and basil (¼ teaspoon each) for sage, allspice, and nutmeg.

SMOKE BURGERS

½ lb ground sirloin
½ small onion, chopped
¼ teaspoon Liquid Smoke
ground pepper to taste
garlic powder to taste
1 tablespoon vegetable oil

Combine all ingredients (except oil) in bowl and knead by hand until well mixed. Heat frying pan over medium flame and add oil. Shape meat mixture into two ½-inch-thick burgers and fry in pan to desired degree of doneness. If you're a cheeseburger nut, melt a thick slice of medium to sharp cheddar over each burger. Serve on a kaiser roll with salad on the side.

Sooner or later you're going to want to get away from the ground-round side of life and step up to a different slice. That's when it gets to be fun.

TOKYO TERIYAKI

½ lb sirloin steak, cut in 1" cubes
⅓ medium onion, chopped
¼ teaspoon ginger
2 oz teriyaki sauce
½ to 1 cup precooked rice
pineapple chunks

Combine steak, onion, ginger, and teriyaki sauce in bowl and marinate for 10 to 15 minutes. Heat frying pan and add steak and marinade. Cook until done. Add a little water if necessary. Push meat and onions to one side of pan. Add precooked rice and heat through. About l minute before serving, add pineapple chunks and heat.

As for the next recipe, let me say thanks to a friend who Thai'd one on!

BANGKOK BEEF'N PEPPERS

½ lb sirloin, cubed
½ cup mushrooms, sliced
¼ teaspoon garlic
½ teaspoon ginger
½ tablespoon sugar
1 tablespoon soy sauce
¼ teaspoon cayenne pepper
1 small onion, chopped
1 small red pepper, cut in strips
1 tablespoon vegetable oil
1 beef bouillon cube dissolved in ¾ cup boiling water
1 teaspoon cornstarch and 1 tablespoon water

In bowl, combine beef, garlic, ginger, sugar, cayenne pepper, and soy sauce. Heat frying pan over high flame until very hot. Add oil and sauté onion and peppers until soft. Add beef and cook until browned. Stir often. Add beef-stock mixture and mushrooms and cook until sauce thickens. (Mix cornstarch and water in cup with whisk and add to thicken sauce.) Serve with precooked rice. I've found that some sliced fresh pineapple on the plate tastes great and helps cut the sting of this dish.

HAIR-RAISIN CURRY BEEF

  ½ cup boiling water
  ½ cup raisins
  1 tablespoon olive oil
  ½ lb sirloin, cut in 1" cubes
  ½ medium onion, chopped
  ½ medium green pepper, chopped
  ½ tablespoon curry powder
  ½ teaspoon salt (optional)
  ⅓ cup unsalted peanuts
  1 beef bouillon cube

In a dish or small bowl, pour boiling water over raisins and set aside. In a frying pan, add oil and brown meat and vegetables over medium heat. Drain oil. Add curry powder and mix well. Mix in salt (if desired) and nuts. Drain raisins (reserve juice); add raisins to meat mixture. To reserved raisin juice, add enough water to measure ½ cup. Add this and bouillon cube to meat mixture and simmer for 15 minutes.

The following is not a recipe for the cholesterol-conscious. However, for a trail-end meal, there are few that can match this one for the fun of cooking and the sheer enjoyment of eating. You do have to be quick with this one. Have all of your ingredients prepped before you start to cook.

STIR-FRY BEEF WITH BUTTER SAUCE

Butter Sauce
2 oz slivered almonds
1 green onion, chopped
1 tablespoon peanut oil
¼ teaspoon curry powder
1 stick butter (margarine OK in a pinch)
juice of 1 lemon
salt and pepper to taste

Preheat frying pan over medium flame. Add oil and brown almonds and onion. Remove from heat and drain. Wipe pan clean. Return nuts and onions to pan and add remaining ingredients. Let butter melt, but do not brown. Stir until well mixed. Remove from pan and set aside in covered bowl.

2 tablespoons peanut oil
½ lb beef, sliced thin
¼ cup green peppers, chopped
¼ cup red peppers, chopped
¼ cup mushrooms, sliced
½ teaspoon salt (optional)
pepper to taste

Heat oil until it smokes. Add meat and quickly brown. Turn regularly to keep from sticking and burning. Add remaining ingredients and quickly stir-fry. Reduce heat and add butter sauce. Toss quickly to coat.

If you'd like a lower-fat version of the above recipe, replace the butter sauce with ¼ cup red wine. You can also omit the butter sauce and go for some soy sauce to make tongues really tingle. By the way, all these variations work well with rice. Remember, precook the rice at home and then pour the freshly cooked food over it to reheat.

SOY SAUCE SIRLOIN

6 oz sirloin, sliced thin
¼ cup peanut oil
3 green onions, sliced in 1" pieces
1 6-oz can water chestnuts, sliced
1 medium green pepper, sliced
2 oz dried pineapple chunks
2 tablespoons cornstarch
¼ cup water
¼ cup soy sauce

Preheat pan and add oil. Sauté beef in hot oil for about 30 seconds on each side. Add remaining ingredients except cornstarch, water, and soy sauce. Cook 4 to 5 minutes over medium flame. Meanwhile, dissolve cornstarch in water. Add cornstarch mixture and soy sauce to pan and stir until thickened.

Feel like a taste of the Old West?

BIG JOHN'S DIXIE-FRIED STEAK

½ lb steak, well marbled
1 tablespoon butter
½ cup water
2 tablespoons flour
salt and pepper to taste

Preheat frying pan over medium flame and melt butter. Add meat and slowly fry steak. Reduce heat as needed to keep from sticking. Once meat is cooked to taste, remove from pan. Add water and slowly stir in flour to make a gravy, carefully scraping pan to remove all meat drippings. Pour gravy over steak. Serve with a raw carrot and hard rolls.

Take a hard left turn at Vladivostok to get to the next flavor classic.

BEEF STROGANOFF

½ lb steak (round or sirloin), cut in 1-inch cubes
3 tablespoons flour
½ cup onion, chopped
3 tablespoons corn oil
1 clove garlic, minced
¼ teaspoon pepper
¼ teaspoon paprika
4 mushrooms, sliced
¼ cup dry red wine or sherry
1 packet dry creamed vegetable soup mix, reconstituted
3 oz cream cheese

Place beef and flour in plastic bag and shake to coat. Heat frying pan over medium to high flame. Add oil. Sauté onions and beef in oil until beef is uniformly browned. Add remaining ingredients except soup and cream cheese. Stir and let simmer for about 5 minutes. Add soup and simmer another 10 minutes. Slice in cream cheese and stir well. Dish out steaming hot over pre-cooked noodles.

Everybody's mother has a recipe for goulash. Mine made it with hamburger and elbow macaroni.

MOM'S GOULASH

⅓ lb hamburger
salt and pepper to taste
1 medium onion, diced
1 medium green pepper, diced
¼ to ½ teaspoon oregano
¼ teaspoon garlic powder
¼ teaspoon basil
½ teaspoon sugar
1 fresh tomato, cubed (optional)
1 6-oz can tomato paste
1 cup water
½ cup precooked macaroni

Heat frying pan over medium flame and brown meat until crumbly. Add salt, pepper, onion, and green pepper and sauté until veggies are soft. Drain off any fat. Return to heat and add remaining ingredients (except macaroni), stirring until tomato paste is dissolved. Simmer for 10 minutes. Add macaroni and stir until hot. Serve with Parmesan cheese and French bread.

But there's another version that's sure to raise a few tent stakes whenever it's served.

PROTEIN-BUSTER GOULASH

1 tablespoon bacon fat (clear)
6 oz sirloin steak, cut in ½" cubes
2 medium onions, chopped
2 stalks celery, sliced
1 package dry tomato soup mix (single-serving size)
¾ cup water
salt, pepper, and paprika to taste
8 oz red kidney beans, drained
flour

Heat frying pan over medium to high flame. Add fat and brown meat until done. Add onions, celery, soup mix, and water. Simmer for 30 minutes. Add beans and seasonings. Thicken sauce with flour as needed.

With all the beef and beans, you won't run short on protein. Serve this with bread and you'll have a meal you can really wrap yourself around.

Dessert

I'll be honest. The frying pan isn't the easiest thing to use if you're trying to cook dessert. That's why I have a favorite fruit-cup recipe.

COCONUTS TO YOU FRUIT CUP

  1 orange, cubed
  1 apple or pear, cubed
  1 banana, sliced (optional)
  ¼ cup shredded coconut
  1 tablespoon sugar (optional)

Mix fruit, coconut, and sugar (if desired) and let rest in a covered dish for 30 minutes. Eat with great joy.

Most cultures do feature pancakes as a favorite dessert. They're usually thin, sweet, and covered with marvelous fruit preserves or powdered sugar. Any pancake batter mix can serve the purpose, but add more water or milk than suggested because you want a thin batter to give you delicate, thin pancakes.

I'm half Swede. So here's a family favorite from the Old Country. If you're French, it's crepes to you. To me, it's plättar.

PLÄTTAR

  1 egg
  ⅔ cup milk
  dash of salt (optional)
  1 tablespoon sugar
  ¼ cup flour
  1 tablespoon vegetable oil

Beat egg well. Add milk, salt, sugar, flour, and oil. Mix thoroughly. Heat oil in frying pan. Cook pancakes on both sides. If batter is too thick, add a little more milk. These

pancakes should be very thin. Serve with powdered sugar
or strawberry preserves.

You can use your frying pan to cook doughnuts, but I
don't recommend it. Two reasons: First, you have to use a
lot of oil (at least 1 cup). That's both heavy to carry and
difficult to dispose of when you're done. Second, and
even more important, you have to bring that oil to a very
high temperature. One slip and you and your trekking
companions will be dealing with a very serious burn. Be
safe, be smart, and keep the deep frying to a minimum.

THE POT

Whereas the recipes for the frying pan were designed for quick cooking, the ones for the pot are meant to be a bit slower to finish, allowing tougher meats to tenderize, pungent flavors to mellow, and tasty sauces to blend into a savory meal.

I've found that meals eaten out of the one-quart pot from my cook kit offer a unique taste experience. Certainly it's a world of stews and soups. But outdoors, you can stroll down the Apian Way or peer out onto the misty moors when you put the pot on the burner.

The boiling point of water drops 9° F with every 5,000 feet in altitude, and in consequence cooking times of boiled foods double at 5,000 feet and quadruple at 10,000 feet. Remember too that some stoves (such as alcohol) cook slower than others. Adjust accordingly.

BREAKFAST

Getting breakfast out of the pot is one quick way to hit the trail. Take a look at some of these favorites.

Cereals

Cereals and other grain dishes are an easy way to get started and give you a lot of get up and go. But as with all meals, you have to build a complete and balanced supply of nutrients. Don't forget the fruit and milk.

OATMEAL EXTRAORDINAIRE

1½ cups water
⅛ teaspoon salt (optional)
⅔ cup old-fashioned oatmeal
½ cup raisins
2 tablespoons brown sugar
¼ cup walnuts

Over a medium flame, bring the water (salt added, if desired) to a boil. Add oats, stirring slowly to prevent lumping. Cook for 5 minutes. Add raisins and cook for another 2 to 3 minutes, stirring occasionally. When ready to eat, stir in brown sugar and walnuts.

CINNAMON-ORANGE CREAM OF WHEAT

2 cups water
¼ teaspoon salt (optional)
⅓ cup Cream of Wheat (original, not quick)
1 teaspoon cinnamon
6-oz can Mandarin orange segments, drained

Over a medium flame, bring water and salt (if desired) to a boil. Add cereal, stirring to prevent lumping. Cook for 7 to 10 minutes, making sure not to burn the cereal. Just before you are ready to eat, add the cinnamon and oranges.

Of course, you can add just about anything you want to a cooked grain mixture. Just follow package directions and then let your imagination run wild. Some of the great taste successes I've tried in my oatmeal are: apple chunks, cinnamon, and nuts; dates and brown sugar; real maple syrup (needs no more help); and applesauce and straw-berries. Most of these additions require no cooking. Just put them in when you're ready to eat. Some, like raisins and apples, need a few minutes in the mix to soften and warm up.

There are at least a dozen different commercial hot cereals to choose from. I've found that the ones labeled "instant" or "quick" sacrifice some of the appeal of the real McCoy, though. Take the time (an extra five minutes or so) to cook up a mix that's really satisfying and packed with energy. By the way, many cold cereals, such as Grape Nuts and Shredded Wheat, can be cooked to make an early-morning tummy warmer.

Morning Beverages

I like coffee. Steaming hot, strong coffee. And I'm not a fanatic who insists that the only real trail coffee is that which has grounds and egg shells floating in it. I use a tea ball.

DON'S TRAIL BREW

(For 2 cups)
2 tablespoons fresh-ground coffee (auto-drip or finer grind)
2 cups water
1 tablespoon sugar
1 teaspoon cinnamon

Bring water to boil. Spoon coffee into tea ball and add to boiling water. Let it brew for 4 to 5 minutes. Remove tea ball. Add sugar and cinnamon. Serve with milk, cream, or whitener if you prefer.

Eggs and Meats

About any way you can cook an egg in a frying pan, you can do in a pot—a bit differently, but cooked nonetheless. It's just more interesting when you go beyond the eggs and start adding meats, for instance.

And that's where you have to change the way you think about how you cook meats.

The vegetable steamer.

For many people, meat isn't properly prepared until there's a charred layer to prove it has passed the trial by fire. But think Oriental for a moment. Meat that has been steamed, not unlike dim sum, is just as well done as if it had been stuck to your frying pan two or three times. That's how I cook my morning meat.

You need only about a half cup of boiling water and a cover for your pot to fix most cuts of meat. However, it's critical that the meat be thawed, especially if it is fresh instead of precooked or leftover. Otherwise you might end up with sausage or steak that is too rare or even dangerously undercooked.

As with all foods, make sure your meat hasn't spoiled before you cook it. You usually can't tell if meat is spoiled just by looking at it, though certainly an "off" smell should tell you something's wrong. But sometimes meat can be bad and not give off any telltale aroma. When in doubt, double-wrap it, pack it out with you, and toss it when you get home. Better a meal without meat than risk food poisoning.

Another caution about steaming involves handling the utensils and steering clear of the steam. You can get an

incredibly nasty burn from steam. Never place the
steamer in a pot of boiling water. Always start with
everything cold—the meat, the steamer, the pan, the
water, even the stove. When you remove the steamer from
the pan, carefully lift the cover off away from your face.
The first thing out of the pot will be live steam (that's
steam under pressure—and it's a lot hotter than 212°F).
Then, let everything cool off for a few moments before
you move in with your hot-pot tongs to remove the
steamer. And now for the recipes.

SAUSAGE LINKS

Uncooked, 10 minutes
"Brown 'n serve," 5 minutes

Place unfrozen links on steamer. Pour ½ cup water in
pan. Put steamer in pan and cover. Over medium flame,
bring water to boil. Time cooking from when water boils.

HAM STICKS

4 oz cooked ham, cut into 4" sticks

Steam until piping hot (about 5–8 minutes). You can
substitute "Spam," but the consistency of the cooked
product will be different from solid ham.

SOY SAUCE STEAK SUNRISE

3 tablespoons soy sauce
1 tablespoon honey
¼ lb sirloin or other lean steak, sliced thin

Mix soy sauce and honey and marinate steak in it for 15
minutes. Discard marinade. Place meat on steamer and
put in pot with ½ cup cold water. Cover and bring water
to boil. Cook meat for 3 minutes (rare) to 6 or 7 minutes
(well done).

AM SAUSAGE BURRITO

  2 flour tortillas
  1 tablespoon peanut oil
  ¼ lb ground sausage
  2 eggs
  diced green pepper and onion (optional)

Rub oil on one side of each tortilla. Roll loosely and place on steamer. Place steamer in pan, add ½ cup water, and bring to boil. Heat tortillas for about 1 minute. Remove pan from heat and remove cover. Once steam clears, remove tortillas and place half of sausage meat in each tortilla on non-oiled side. Fold tortilla over meat so that it resembles a small pillow. Place back on steamer, folded part down. Bring water level back to ½ cup and place steamer inside. Cover and bring to boil over medium heat. Time for 15 minutes once water boils. Put two eggs alongside tortillas on steamer to hardboil for a solid beginning on breakfast. To spice up the burrito, add some diced green pepper and onion to meat before placing it in tortilla.

A great staple of any wilderness breakfast is the common chicken egg, though you can also use duck or goose eggs to fill out your morning plate.

Many of us think of eggs and frying pans as inseparable. Unfortunately that's too often the case, especially when we forget the margarine. But eggs in a pot have a noble history, reaching back into the smoky past of cast-iron cauldrons bubbling over a few chunks of aspen or chestnut.

You can always treat your pot like a frying pan and make scrambled eggs, but I want to talk about ways to turn the benefits of the pot to your eggs' advantage.

HARD-BOILED EGGS

2 large eggs
1 to 1½ cups water
¼ teaspoon salt

Pour water in pan with salt (if desired). Bring water to boil over medium to high flame. Reduce heat so water is just barely bubbling. Add eggs. Maintain flame so that water keeps boiling very slowly. Cook eggs too fast and they'll crack and ooze. Boil for about 5 to 7 minutes. At higher altitudes (up to about 10,000 feet), cook 10 to 12 minutes. Remove eggs with spoon and set aside to cool (soak in bowl of cold water). Peel and eat.

Hard-boiled eggs are versatile. You can peel and eat them au naturel. You can slice and sprinkle them with salt and pepper, grated cheese, diced chives or onions, or pine nuts and Parmesan. You can also do a bit more with hard-boiled eggs while still in the pot.

EGGS À LA GOLDENROD

2 to 3 hard-boiled eggs
¼ cup flour
½ cup milk (or powdered milk and water in 1:3 ratio)
½ to 1 cup water
white pepper
1 or 2 slices of bread

Peel eggs and separate yolks from whites. Slice whites and set aside. Over a medium flame, heat milk in pot. Do not boil. In a bowl, add water a bit at a time to flour to make a paste. Slowly add paste to milk to make white sauce (stir as mixture thickens). Add sliced egg whites. Add white pepper to taste. Heat mixture through and spoon over bread. Mash yolks and sprinkle over top.

The most popular way to cook eggs in a pot, besides boiling them, is poaching them. Poaching eggs on the trail isn't hard, it just takes a bit of wrist action.

POACHED EGGS

2 cups water
¼ cup white vinegar
2 or 3 large eggs

Over a medium to high flame, bring water to a boil and add vinegar. With a spoon, stir liquid to create a whirlpool. Add eggs to whirlpool while continuing to swirl the water. This will roll the eggs and keep them from spreading out. Every 15 to 20 seconds, reverse the direction of the whirlpool by rocking the pan in the opposite direction. After about 3 minutes, remove the eggs from the pan. Serve over bread, rolls, or hot hash.

Poached eggs are the base for the king of all egg dishes—Eggs Benedict. Simply speaking, this is poached eggs on top of sliced Canadian bacon and English muffins, covered with Hollandaise sauce. It's possible to make Hollandaise sauce in the woods, but you need a double boiler. That's a bit much for the one-pan chef.

I suggest substituting a spruced-up white sauce.

WHITE SAUCE FOR POACHED EGGS

¼ cup milk (or powdered milk and water in 1:3 ratio)
2 tablespoons flour
¼ cup water
1 tablespoon margarine
salt and pepper to taste
Parmesan cheese (optional)

Mix flour and water in bowl to form paste. Heat milk in pot over medium flame. Add margarine to melt, stirring frequently. Add flour mixture gradually to thicken sauce. Add salt and pepper. Continue to heat until sauce is thick. Set aside and cover. Serve over poached eggs placed on slice of ham or Canadian bacon on top of sliced English muffin to make mock Eggs Benedict. For some added flavor, stir in a healthy dash of grated cheese.

LUNCH AND DINNER

Turning your only pot into a vat of earthly delights is easy if you're willing to take a little time. I've always found that cooking in a pot offers a totally different experience from cooking in a frying pan. The pot is a world of spices and sauces, of subtle differences in flavor, where gentle nuances bring new blendings of taste to the outdoor scene.

A pot-based meal should be cooked slowly. You have to accept the fact that patience is the critical factor in melding meats, vegetables, seasonings, and liquids into more than an uninspired soup or stew. You can expect to spend 30 or more minutes cooking after the preparation is done. But the wait will be worth it.

Poultry

I prefer to cook with chicken breast, but you can use any part of the bird—legs, thighs, whatever—in these recipes. You can substitute other poultry, if you like, but use caution. Turkey dark meat (legs, thighs) has a stronger flavor than chicken and will yield a different result. I suggest you use turkey breast if you want to substitute. Duck is notoriously greasy, so I avoid it.

Chicken is great because it cooks quickly, it's lean (if you take care to strip away the fat), it's packed with nutrition, and it goes with just about anything you can carry (or dig out of the fridge).

ICEBOX CHICKEN WITH STUFFING

½ lb chicken breast, boned and cubed
3 tablespoons margarine
1 medium onion, diced
½ cup green pepper, chopped
1 small tomato, diced
1 stalk celery, chopped
salt and pepper to taste

1 chicken bouillon cube
½ cup water
½ cup seasoned croutons, or stuffing mix, or Minute Rice
½ teaspoon poultry seasoning if you use Minute Rice

Over a medium flame, heat pot. Melt margarine in pot and sauté vegetables until tender. Add chicken and cook until meat is done. Add salt and pepper, bouillon cube, and water. Continue cooking until cube is dissolved. Add the croutons and stir into mixture until liquid is absorbed and croutons are soft. If you substitute Minute Rice for the croutons, cover the pot and let it sit off the heat for a few minutes. Cooking time will vary depending on the stove and altitude.

Here's a similar theme, but with a slightly different taste and look.

POTTED CHICKEN

1 carrot, cut in chunks
½ stalk celery, sliced
½ medium onion, sliced
1 potato, diced
1 chicken bouillon cube
½ cup water
2 chicken breasts, boned
salt and pepper to taste
dried basil to taste

Note: As sold at most counters, two chicken breasts really means one breast cut in half to look something like a Valentine heart. In pot, place all vegetables, bouillon, and water. Bring to a boil over medium flame. Reduce heat and stir. Place chicken on top of veggies, season with salt, pepper, and basil. Cover and continue to cook over low flame for 30 minutes or until chicken is done. Add water as needed to keep broth level up.

The great thing about chicken is that it doesn't color the flavor of the dish as strongly as red meats do. That lets you do some fun things with sauces and vegetables that might otherwise vanish in competition.

RED AND GREEN CHICKEN

½ lb chicken breast, boned and cubed
2 tablespoons margarine
1 small onion, diced
½ tablespoon paprika
½ teaspoon salt (optional)
pepper to taste
1 medium green pepper, diced
1 medium red pepper, diced
¾ cup water
4 oz cream cheese

Over medium flame, heat pot. Melt margarine and brown onions. Add paprika and chicken and cook over low heat for about 20 minutes. Add water, salt, pepper, and remaining veggies. Cover and cook for another 15–20 minutes, stirring occasionally. Add cream cheese, a lump at a time, until it melts and mixes into the sauce. Serve with chunks of sourdough or other heavy grain bread. It really goes well with pasta, which you can precook at home.

The next item can work either as a complement to a meal or as a quick stand alone for lunch.

TASTY PASTA WITH CHEESE

4 oz pasta (2 good handfuls), uncooked
1 tablespoon olive oil
1 teaspoon vegetable oil
¼ teaspoon hot pepper flakes
Salt and pepper to taste
1 handful shelled walnuts or pine nuts
¼ cup any grated cheese

In salted boiling water, cook pasta until done. Drain and return to pot. Add all other ingredients. Gently toss.

HOT 'N STEAMY CHICKEN

1 or 2 chicken legs
1 large carrot, peeled and sliced
1 large potato, peeled and sliced
1 medium green pepper, sliced into spears
1 tablespoon light brown sugar
salt, pepper and curry powder to taste
3 tablespoons water

Place vegetables in pot. Combine curry powder, salt, pepper, and brown sugar. Coat chicken with this mixture. Place chicken on top of vegetables. Add water and cover pan. Cook over medium flame about 40 minutes. Check to make sure water doesn't evaporate. Add liquid as needed to avoid burning. Scrape veggies away from pan if they begin to stick, but don't stir mixture.

CALCUTTA CHICKEN

½ lb chicken breast, boned and cubed
4 tablespoons butter or margarine
1 medium onion, finely chopped
1 stalk celery, finely chopped
⅓ cup flour
2 chicken bouillon cubes dissolved in 1½ cups water
1 6-oz can tomato juice
½ teaspoon Worcestershire sauce
1 teaspoon curry powder
precooked rice

Over medium flame, melt the margarine and sauté vegetables until tender. Add chicken and cook, stirring occasionally. Add flour and stir to mix. Add bouillon cubes and water immediately and cook until sauce is smooth and thick. Add tomato juice, curry powder, and Worcestershire. Cover and simmer for 5 minutes. Serve over precooked rice.

BARCELONA BIRD

½ lb chicken breast, boned and cubed
2 tablespoons margarine
1 large tomato, cubed
1 medium green pepper, diced
1 medium onion, chopped
1 6-oz can tomato paste
¾ cup water
¼ teaspoon cayenne pepper
salt and pepper to taste
¾ cup Minute Rice (optional)
¼ cup black olives, diced (optional)

Over medium flame, heat pot and melt margarine. Add chicken and cook for 10 minutes. Add veggies and sauté until chicken is tender. Add the remaining ingredients except rice and olives. Simmer sauce to very slow bubbling boil. Add rice and stir into mix. Cover and set aside for 5 minutes. Sprinkle with olives, if desired.

Keeping the international flavor, let's cross the Mediterranean and take a stroll along the Apian Way.

COLOSSAL CHICKEN

1 tablespoon olive oil
2 chicken breasts, boned and cut in chunks (see note in
        Potted Chicken recipe, page 81)
1 medium onion, diced
1 clove garlic, crushed
3 large mushrooms, sliced
1 6-oz can tomato paste
1 cup water
1 fresh but very ripe tomato, crushed
½ teaspoon oregano
¼ teaspoon each basil, black pepper, fennel seed
1 teaspoon sugar
1 tablespoon Parmesan cheese
precooked spaghetti

Over medium flame, heat oil in pot. Brown chicken, turning to prevent sticking. Add vegetables and sauté until tender. Add remaining ingredients except pasta. Stir until tomato paste dissolves. Reduce heat, cover, and cook for about 30 minutes. Balance seasonings as you wish. Serve with precooked spaghetti.

Try the above recipe without chicken for a powerful spaghetti sauce. Consider crumbling a bay leaf and dicing up green peppers to amplify the aroma and enhance the appearance.

Friends have asked me about the old Saturday night favorite, franks and beans. I've said many times that hot dogs are an easy way out of having to think when you're cooking. However, the beans are another story.

BOSTON BASTED BIRD

 1 chicken breast, boned (see note in Potted Chicken recipe, page 81)
 3 strips thick-cut bacon
 1 12-ounce can baked beans, drained and repackaged into plastic
 ½ cup raisins
 1 tablespoon brown sugar

Wrap bacon around chicken breast. Heat pot over medium flame and brown meat. Cook for about 10 minutes, turning to keep from burning. Drain off excess grease. Combine baked beans, raisins, and brown sugar. Pour mixture over chicken and bacon, making sure the meat is well covered. Simmer over low heat, covered, about 25 minutes. Serve with brown bread. *Note: This can also be prepared as a casserole for use in the oven. Follow the recipe to the point of simmering over low heat, and instead place in oven pan, cover, and bake 1 hour at medium heat.*

CHICAGO-STYLE CHICKEN

   3 tablespoons flour
   1 tablespoon dry mustard
   1 teaspoon pepper
   2 chicken breasts, boned and cut in strips (see note in
        Potted Chicken recipe, page 81)
   1 medium onion, chopped
   2 tablespoons vegetable oil
   1 cup water
   ½ packet powdered milk (1-quart size packet)
   1 tablespoon flour
   1 tomato, sliced thin
   1 tablespoon fresh parsley, chopped
   1 stalk celery, chopped
   1 dill pickle, chopped (optional)

Combine flour, mustard, and pepper in plastic bag and
shake chicken in it to coat. In pot, heat oil and brown
chicken, turning to avoid burning. Add onion and sauté
until tender. Mix water and milk powder. Add flour to
reconstituted milk and add to pot, heating to a boil (do
not burn). Add tomato, parsley, and celery. Reduce heat,
cover and cook for 20 to 25 minutes or until chicken is
cooked. Stir to prevent sticking. Serve with hard roll, and
garnish with a chopped dill pickle, if desired.

If you like mushrooms, you're sure to like this recipe.

MUSHED CHICKEN

   ½ tablespoon vegetable oil
   ½ cup mushrooms, sliced
   ½ medium onion, finely chopped
   2 chicken bouillon cubes
   1 cup water
   2 chicken breasts, boned (see note in Potted Chicken

recipe, page 81)
oregano to taste
pepper to taste
½ cup Minute Rice, uncooked
1 carrot, cut in thin curls

In pot over medium flame, heat oil and sauté mushrooms and onions. When vegetables are tender, add water and bouillon cubes. Bring to boil. Reduce heat and place chicken on top of vegetables. Season with oregano and pepper. Cover and cook for 35 minutes. Remove chicken and add rice. Stir to mix. Return chicken to pot. Drop carrots on top of all. Cover and cook another 5 minutes. Remove pot from stove and let sit 5 minutes before removing cover.

This next dish goes great over noodles or French bread.

CHICKEN 'N GREEN-EYED GRAVY

1 tablespoon vegetable oil
2 chicken breasts, boned and cut in chunks (see note in Potted Chicken, page 81)
1 medium onion, chopped
¾ cup water
1 chicken bouillon cube
¾ cup freeze-dried peas
salt and pepper to taste
flour and water to thicken

Heat pot over medium flame. Add oil and brown chicken. Add onion and cook until soft. Add all other ingredients except flour and cook for about 30 minutes or until peas are soft. Add water as needed. Thicken gravy by making paste of water and flour and stirring in slowly to prevent lumps.

The search for flavor being the mother of invention, here's a quick and easy way to tickle your taste buds.

CREAMED CHICKEN AND NOODLES

  2 chicken bouillon cubes
  1½ cups water
  1 chicken breast, boned and cut in chunks
  3 oz cream cheese
  ½ cup freeze-dried peas
  2 tablespoons flour
  1 red pepper, diced
  1 cup noodles or macaroni, precooked

In pot, bring bouillon cubes and water to boil. Add all other ingredients (add cheese a chunk at a time). Reduce heat, cover, and simmer for 30 minutes. Stir occasionally. Serve over precooked noodles.

This next recipe is about as simple as you can get in a pot. You do, however, have to carry the bones out after enjoying this dish in the wild.

OLD FASHIONED CHICKEN FRICASSEE

  2 chicken legs, disjointed
  ¾ cup water (approximate)
  1½ teaspoons flour
  ¾ cup milk (or powdered milk and water in 1:3 ratio)
  salt and pepper to taste

Place chicken legs in pot and add just enough water to cover. Cook over medium flame for 35 to 45 minutes or until meat begins coming off bones. (There should be at least ½ cup of liquid left in pot.) Mix milk and flour together and add to pot. Bring to boil, gently stirring to prevent sticking. Salt and pepper as you wish. Serve over precooked noodles or biscuits. Fresh carrot sticks will fill out the meal.

Don't think you have to put your pot over the flame to make a sumptuous meal. Try this one on for size.

TASTY CHICKEN SALAD

½ lb chicken, precooked and diced
2 tablespoons honey
2 tablespoons vegetable oil
juice of 1 lemon
¼ teaspoon onion salt (optional)
1 stalk celery, diced
3 packets mustard (or 1½ teaspoons)
1 cup chop suey noodles

In pot, whisk all ingredients except chicken and noodles. Add chicken and noodles and toss to coat.

Soups and Stews

When archaeologists examine the human record, they often evaluate civilizations based on the decorations found on potshards turned up in the diggings. To me that says one thing—the ancients knew the pot was more than just a water-gathering device. It was the center of the home, the symbol of the hearth that provided for all who clustered around.

Over the years, soups and stews have been a mainstay in the wilderness menu. The ingredients are relatively easy to carry, since the heaviest is the one you dip out of a lake. And you can make a lot of soup quickly. I've found that the best time for a soup or stew is when the wind is cutting and I need warming up fast. Melting a few pots of snow and tossing in a handful of vegetables, seasonings, and meat leaves me ample time to get a tent pitched and gear readied. Then it's time to eat!

For the Basic Soup recipe, you can combine all the dry

ingredients in a bag at home. Then all you have to do is dump them into the boiling water without taking time to measure.

BASIC SOUP

 2½ cups water
 3 bouillon cubes (chicken or beef)
 1 tablespoon oil (optional)
 ½ lb meat (optional)
 1 small tomato, 2 to 3 tablespoons tomato paste, or
   small handful of dried tomatoes
 1 carrot, chopped (freeze-dried is OK)
 1 handful freeze-dried peas
 1 handful freeze-dried potatoes
 ½ teaspoon celery seeds
 1 tablespoon dried parsley
 1 tablespoon dried onion flakes
 pepper to taste
 garlic powder to taste

In pot over medium flame, heat oil and brown meat. Do not burn. Add water and bouillon cubes. Bring to a boil and add all other ingredients. Reduce heat and cover. Simmer for about 25 to 30 minutes.

FAST PEA SOUP

 2½ cups water
 ¼ teaspoon salt (optional)
 1 cup freeze-dried peas (more for thicker soup)
 ½ cup ham, diced
 1 carrot, diced
 ½ teaspoon thyme

In pot over medium flame, bring salted water to boil. Add all ingredients and cover. Simmer for about 45 minutes or longer to cook down peas, stirring occasionally. Serve with soda crackers or bread.

This next soup was inspired by those hardy souls who paddled the North Country in search of furs during the 18th and 19th centuries. It takes a long time to cook, so keep it for a layover day on your trip.

VOYAGEUR PEA SOUP

 2 cups water (or more)
 1 cup dried (not freeze-dried) yellow or green peas
 1 medium onion, diced
 ½ cup ham, diced
 salt and pepper to taste
 1 to 2 tablespoons flour

Soak dried peas in water for about 6 hours. When ready to cook, add water to bring to 2 cups. Add salt (if desired) and bring to boil over medium flame, stirring to prevent sticking. Add ham and onion. Cover and reduce heat. Cook for at least 1 hour, adding flour to thicken if desired.

Sometimes familiar territory tastes best when your stomach asks if the soup's on.

DON'S PENICILLIN

 1 chicken leg, disjointed
 2½ cups water
 ½ teaspoon salt (optional)
 2 carrots, diced
 1 tablespoon onion flakes
 pepper to taste
 1 bay leaf
 ¼ teaspoon thyme
 ½ cup noodles, uncooked

In pot over medium flame, bring salted water to gentle boil. Cook chicken leg until meat falls off bone (this will take upwards of 45 minutes) adding water as needed. Remove bones and add all other ingredients except noodles. Cook another 25 minutes or until carrots are cooked. Add noodles and cook until tender.

The wonders of chicken soup are legendary. Yet for me, the ultimate chicken soup has to be a major meal in a bowl. And that means chicken stew.

SOUPER CLUCK STEW

2½ cups water (or more)
1 chicken breast, precooked and cut in chunks
3 chicken bouillon cubes
2 potatoes, peeled and diced
1 carrot, chopped
1 medium onion, chopped
¼ teaspoon cayenne pepper
1 clove garlic, crushed
¼ teaspoon pepper
1 small tomato, quartered
½ cup dried corn
flour (optional)

Place all ingredients except corn and tomato in pot over medium to high flame. Bring to boil, cover, and reduce heat. Simmer 30 minutes. Add corn and tomato and continue to simmer another 15 minutes. Add water as needed. Thicken with flour if needed.

CHOW-HOUND CHOWDER

1 chicken breast, precooked and chopped
2 cups water
½ cup dried corn
¼ cup onion flakes
1 stalk celery, chopped
1 packet dried nonfat milk (1-qt size, or 1⅓ cups)
2 to 3 tablespoons flour
salt and pepper to taste

In pot, mix all ingredients except flour. Heat over medium flame until corn is rehydrated. If thickening is needed, mix flour with a few tablespoons of water to make a paste. Stir well while adding this to stew to prevent lumps.

Instead of "cluck," you might want "moo" in your meal. If so, take a shot at a high-powered soup that's got more mulligan in it than a 6:45 A.M. Saturday tee time.

BIG-TIME BEEF STEW

½ lb stew beef, cut in 1" cubes
1 cup flour
2 to 3 tablespoons vegetable oil
2 cups water
2 medium potatoes, cubed (leave skin on)
1 medium onion, cut in chunks
2 carrots, cut in chunks
salt and pepper to taste
1 bay leaf
1 teaspoon Worcestershire sauce
celery seed to taste
1 egg, beaten

Place flour in bowl and dredge meat in flour. Over medium flame, heat pot and add oil. Brown floured meat, turning to prevent sticking. Save leftover flour. Add water to pot and scrape with spoon. Add all other ingredients, cover, and simmer at least 30 minutes. Stir occasionally. Add a little water, a few dashes of vegetable oil, and the beaten egg to remaining flour. Mix into a sticky dough. With oiled spoon, drop balls of dough into stew, cover pan again, and cook 5 more minutes. *Do not stir* stew after you add the dumplings.

Here's a vegetarian stew from Chris Townsend, author of *The Backpacker's Handbook* (Ragged Mountain Press, 1993).

CARROT AND LENTIL STEW

   ½ cup lentils
   1 large carrot, diced
   1 medium onion, diced
   1 garlic clove, crushed
   1 large tomato
   1 teaspoon parsley
   1 bay leaf
   pinch of salt
   black pepper to taste
   chili powder to taste (optional)

Add lentils and vegetables to 4 cups cold water (more if you prefer a soupy stew), bring to a boil, then simmer 45 minutes or until lentils are soft. Add salt after cooking (adding it before slows down cooking). Cooking time can be shortened if lentils are soaked beforehand in hot water. Serve with wholegrain bread.

Vegetables

And speaking of vegetarian dishes, here are a few recipes to make your trail meal greener and tastier. For a hearty pasta dish, try the Pasta and Sauce (page 103) without the beef. For a good ratatouille, try the recipe on page 102, substituting mushrooms for the meat. And for other vegetable dishes, turn to Chapter Four and treat your pot like a pan.

VERY GREEN STUFFED PEPPERS

1 large onion, half diced, other half sliced ¼-inch thick
¾ cup wild rice, precooked
½ cup Minute Rice, precooked
1 medium tomato, diced
¼ cup seasoned bread crumbs
1 egg, beaten
4 to 6 oz cheddar cheese, grated
¼ cup green olives with pimentos, chopped
salt and pepper to taste
2 medium green peppers
½ cup water

In bowl, mix all ingredients except peppers and onion slices. Cut top off each pepper and clean out seeds. Stuff peppers. Place onion slices on bottom of pot. Place peppers on top of onions. Add water and cover. Over a medium flame, bring water to boil and cook peppers 45 minutes.

SPAGHETTI WITH CHEESE AND TOMATO SAUCE

8 oz spaghetti or noodles
1 large tin of tomatoes
Parmesan cheese or other hard cheese, diced or
    grated—as much as you like!
1 large onion, sliced
1 garlic clove, crushed
pinch of mixed herbs
black pepper to taste

Boil lots of water in your pot. Add spaghetti and onion. Boil uncovered for ten minutes or until spaghetti is cooked, stirring occasionally. Drain off water. Add tomatoes, cheese, garlic, and herbs and return to heat, stirring constantly until cheese has melted.

"IT'S ALL WE HAD IN THE DEPRESSION" TOMATO LUNCH

3 large tomatoes
2¼ cups water, divided
1 green pepper, diced
1 onion, diced
2 tablespoons sugar
salt and pepper to taste
½ cup Minute Rice, uncooked

In pot, bring 2 cups water to boil. Scald tomatoes by dipping them in water with slotted spoon for 30 seconds to 1 minute. Remove from water and peel. Empty water from pot. Return tomatoes to pot and add ¼ cup water. Cover and cook over low flame for 20 minutes. Add all other ingredients and cook another 10 to 15 minutes, stirring to prevent sticking.

RIB STICKIN' POTATO SALAD

2 cups water
2 large potatoes, peeled and quartered
2 eggs
¼ cup green onion, diced
3 tablespoons salad dressing
1 tablespoon prepared mustard
salt and pepper to taste
1 cup mushrooms, sliced (optional)

Boil water in pot and cook potatoes and eggs for 25 minutes. Drain and cut potatoes into small chunks. Dice eggs. Mix all remaining ingredients in pot. For still more protein, add mushrooms.

Here's another from Chris Townsend.

RICE CURRY

1 tablespoon vegetable oil
½ cup brown rice
1 medium onion, sliced
½ teaspoon curry powder (more or less to taste)
1½ cups water
½ cup mushrooms
¼ cup of raisins
1 green pepper, chopped
1 large tomato
1 vegetable bouillon cube

In pot over medium flame, heat oil. Add rice, onion, and curry powder and sauté 1 minute, stirring constantly. Then add 1½ cups water plus the mushrooms, green pepper, raisins, and any other ingredients. Bring to boil then simmer, covered, until all the water has been absorbed (about 30 minutes). White rice can be used. It cooks in half the time but the result won't be as tasty or as nutritious.

Here's an unusual dish that makes a great cold lunch.
Top it off with fruit.

CHILLED SESAME LINGUINE

½ lb thin linguine (#17) or spaghetti
1 tablespoon peanut oil
1 teaspoon minced fresh gingerroot
4 teaspoons sugar
2 tablespoons creamy peanut butter
2 tablespoons soy sauce
1 tablespoon wine vinegar
¼ teaspoon crushed red pepper flakes
2 scallions, cut into 2-inch pieces

Cook linguine in a large pot; drain. Toss with peanut oil
and set aside to cool. In a small bowl, using a wire whisk,
combine ginger with remaining ingredients except scallions. Pour over chilled linguine. Before serving, toss well
and sprinkle scallions over the top.

Meat

Your pot gives you a chance to experiment with beef in
ways you just can't do in a frying pan. The simple fact is
that depending on the cut, beef can be tough and stringy.
Cheap cuts cooked in a frying pan can mean tough times
when the dinner bell rings.

The pot helps solve that problem. Since you will be
cooking the meat for more than 30 minutes in most cases,
you can use chuck or round where you might otherwise
want sirloin. The extended cooking will help tenderize the
cheaper cuts, and that means you can go easy on your
purse while building a meal that goes easy on your
tongue.

Beef has a stronger flavor than poultry and will support
more heady combinations of spices. Don't be afraid to
experiment. Beef also provides a dark gravy that presents
well against starches such as potatoes, noodles, and rice.

BASIC BEEF IN A POT

½ lb bottom round, boneless and cut in strips
3 tablespoons flour
2 tablespoons vegetable oil

Choose one of the following sauces:

Red Sauce
1 green pepper, diced
½ cup water
1 large tomato, crushed
1 teaspoon onion flakes
¼ teaspoon paprika
salt and pepper to taste

Cream Sauce
3 large mushrooms, sliced
1 medium potato, sliced thin
1 cup water
⅔ cup powdered milk or 1 cup milk
1 tablespoon flour
pepper to taste

Brown Sauce
1 carrot, chopped
1 tablespoon sugar
1 cup water
1 tablespoon flour
1 teaspoon onion flakes
¼ teaspoon garlic powder
salt and pepper to taste

In a plastic bag, shake beef in flour until coated. In pot over medium flame, heat oil and brown meat, taking care not to burn meat. For the Red Sauce, add green pepper and sauté until tender, adding extra oil if needed. For the Cream Sauce variation, sauté mushrooms and potatoes. For the Brown Sauce recipe, sauté carrot and add sugar to caramelize both the vegetable and the beef.

At this point, add all other ingredients for sauce base selected. Reduce heat and cover. Cook between 35 and 45 minutes, stirring occasionally to prevent sticking. Add water to keep sauce reduction to a minimum. Serve over noodles or rice or with rolls. If you didn't bring precooked noodles or rice, you can add it before the final 35- to 45-minute simmering. Just be sure you have enough liquid left to cook the starch—add more if necessary. An uncooked vegetable as a side dish will fill out the meal.

No doubt you've figured out that the pot, like the frying pan, is a great way to take a trip around the world. Sort of like taking one trek and then adding another to it.

GARIBALDI'S ROAST BEEF

½ lb Boston roast
2 teaspoons olive oil
½ teaspoon garlic powder
½ teaspoon basil
2 tablespoons prepared mustard
2 tablespoons olive oil
1 cup water
1 medium green pepper, cut in strips
1 large potato, sliced (leave skin on)
1 medium sweet red pepper, cut in strips
1 onion, chopped

Rub oil, garlic powder, basil, and mustard on roast. Heat pot over medium flame and add oil. Brown meat on all sides. Add water, cover, and cook about 1 hour. Add vegetables. Cover and cook another 30 minutes. Serve with Italian roll.

PEDRO'S RICE

½ lb ground beef
1 medium onion, chopped
1 small to medium green pepper, chopped
3 plum tomatoes, crushed
½ cup water
¾ cup rice (raw)
½ teaspoon chili powder
salt and pepper to taste

In pot over medium flame, brown meat until crumbly and drain off grease. Add all other ingredients and stir thoroughly. Bring to moderate boil. Cover, reduce heat, and cook about 20 minutes or until rice is tender.

"SAFE" CHILI

½ lb sirloin, cut in bite-sized chunks
1 teaspoon vegetable oil
1 large onion, chopped
1 clove garlic, crushed
1 medium tomato, chopped
4 large mushrooms, sliced
½ cup dehydrated corn
1 6-oz can tomato paste
¾ cup water
1½ teaspoons chili powder
¼ teaspoon pepper
¼ teaspoon ground cumin
salt to taste

In pot over medium flame, heat oil and brown meat. Add all other ingredients. Cover and simmer until corn is tender.

Normally, the following recipe uses vegetables alone. I've found that beef makes an interesting taste difference, however. You can use only vegetables by substituting 2 cups of sliced mushrooms for the meat.

BEEF RATATOUILLE

½ lb round steak, sliced thin
4 tablespoons olive oil
1 medium onion, sliced
1 clove garlic, crushed
1 green pepper, diced
1 summer squash or zucchini, sliced
1 medium eggplant, diced
1 medium tomato, cut in chunks
1 6-oz can tomato paste
1 cup water
2 to 3 tablespoons sugar
1 bay leaf
¼ teaspoon fennel seed
salt and pepper to taste
Parmesan or Romano cheese (optional)

In pot over medium flame, heat oil. Brown meat, add onions, and sauté until onions are soft. Add all other ingredients. Cover and reduce heat. Stir often. Cook about 35 minutes or until sauce thickens. Add grated Parmesan or Romano cheese.

Here is another version of an old-time favorite.

MEATY STUFFED PEPPERS

½ lb ground beef
1 large onion, half diced, other half sliced ¼-inch thick
⅔ cup Minute Rice, uncooked
1 medium tomato, diced
1 egg, beaten
¼ teaspoon hot pepper sauce
garlic salt and pepper to taste

2 medium green peppers
½ cup water

In bowl, mix all ingredients except peppers and onion slices. Cut top off each pepper and remove seeds. Divide stuffing evenly and pack each pepper. Place onion slices on bottom of pot. Place peppers upright in pot on top of onion slices, add water, and cover. Over medium flame, bring water to boil. Cook 45 minutes. Check to keep water level at least 1 inch up on peppers.

Sticking with good ground beef for a moment, here's another old-time favorite that's super easy when you're toting a pot.

PASTA AND SAUCE

½ lb ground beef
1 tablespoon olive oil
1 onion, diced
1 clove garlic, crushed
1 green pepper, diced
1 large tomato, crushed
1 6-oz can tomato paste
1 cup water
1 teaspoon oregano
½ teaspoon basil
1 tablespoon sugar
1 tablespoon Parmesan cheese
salt and pepper to taste
1 to 1½ cups precooked pasta

In pot over low flame, brown ground beef. Drain and add oil. Heat over medium flame. Add onion, garlic, and green pepper and sauté with meat until tender. Add remaining ingredients, stirring to mix evenly. Simmer 25 minutes. Mix in precooked pasta. Remove from heat and serve with Caesar salad. For a vegetarian dish, omit the meat.

A traditional pot recipe comes to us from the farms and chateaus of France.

DRUNKEN BEEF

½ lb sirloin, cut in 1-inch chunks
flour
1 tablespoon oil or margarine
1 medium onion, chopped
1 clove garlic, finely diced
1 package mushroom soup (single-serving size)
1 cup water
salt and pepper to taste
¼ cup dry red wine
1 to 1½ cups precooked noodles

Dredge meat in flour. Add oil to pot heating over a medium flame. Brown beef. Add onion and garlic and sauté until tender. Add all other ingredients. Bring to boil. Reduce heat, cover, and simmer 35 minutes. Serve over precooked noodles.

Other traditions can be found closer to home. You might want to bring a 2-quart pot if this is going to be Saturday night dinner.

CORNED BEEF À LA MICHAEL

½ lb corned beef, rinsed and tightly wrapped
water
¼ head cabbage
1 large onion, quartered
2 medium potatoes, peeled and cut in half
2 carrots, cut in chunks
½ teaspoon celery flakes
1 bay leaf
pepper to taste

In pot, cover meat with water and simmer about 1 hour,

making sure that water does not boil off. Drain water and add all other ingredients. Cover meat and vegetables with fresh water. Bring to gentle boil, reduce heat, and cover. Cook over low flame about 1 hour.

TICK-TOCK MINUTE STEAK

1 or 2 cube steaks (about ½ lb)
salt and pepper to taste
garlic powder to taste
1 medium onion, sliced
½ cup Minute Rice, uncooked
½ cup cut fresh green beans
1 6-oz can tomato paste
1 cup water

Season meat with salt, pepper, and garlic powder. Layer ingredients in pot: onion, then meat, then rice, then beans. Combine water and tomato paste and pour over everything. Cover and cook over medium heat 30 minutes.

BEEF À LA MACARTHUR

¼ lb dried beef
1 cup water
1 cup milk (made from powdered milk)
2 to 3 tablespoons flour
2 hard-boiled eggs, chopped
salt and pepper to taste

In pot over medium flame, bring meat and water to boil. Cook about 5 minutes. Remove from heat and drain off water. Add milk and return to heat. Warm, but *do not boil.* Slowly stir in flour to thicken sauce. Add eggs and season with salt and pepper. Cook no more than 5 more minutes. Serve over a split hard roll.

The crowning achievement for beef in a pot is just that—the all-American pot roast.

RED, WHITE, AND BROWN POT ROAST

½ lb pot roast
1½ cups water
2 beef bouillon cubes
2 medium potatoes, peeled and quartered
2 carrots, sliced
1 large onion, cut in chunks
salt and pepper to taste

In pot over medium flame, quickly brown meat on all sides. Immediately add remaining ingredients and simmer over medium flame 45 minutes or longer. Stir occasionally to keep from sticking.

Beyond beef are pork and ham. All too often I've heard the complaint that pork is too dry. In the pot, it won't be.

PEASANT PORK CHOPS

2 stalks celery, chopped
1 medium onion, cut in chunks
2 carrots, cut in chunks
1 potato, quartered
1 large tomato, crushed
1 turnip, peeled and cut in chunks
1½ cups water
½ teaspoon salt (optional)
1 beef bouillon cube
1 bay leaf
¼ teaspoon thyme
pepper to taste
2 center-cut loin chops

Combine all vegetables and seasonings with water in pot. Lay chops on top. Cook over a medium flame for 1 hour.

BIG MO CHOPS

2 center-cut loin chops, thick cut
1 medium onion, sliced
1 medium green pepper, cut in strips
1 large potato, sliced
3 packets ketchup (or 1 tablespoon)
2 tablespoons molasses
2 tablespoons water

In pot over medium flame, brown chops. Remove from pot and drain off fat. Place sliced onion in bottom of pot. Lay meat on onion, and other vegetables on top of meat. Cover with ketchup and molasses. Drizzle water over top. Cover and cook 40 minutes over low heat. Add additional water if sauce is too thick.

And what about bacon? It isn't just for breakfast anymore.

BELLY BUSTIN' SPUDS

½ lb bacon, diced
1 medium onion, chopped
1 medium green pepper, chopped
1 stalk celery, chopped
2 large potatoes, sliced
¼ cup fresh parsley, chopped

In pot over medium flame, cook bacon. Do not drain. Add onions, peppers, and celery. Sauté until tender. Add potatoes, stir, and reduce heat. Stir occasionally. After 30 minutes, add parsley. Cook until potatoes start to fall apart.

Dessert

Compotes, puddings, baked fruits—all are taste delights sure to top off a great meal. Your pot is the perfect venue for flavor and fun.

INDIAN PUDDING

1 can sweetened condensed milk
½ cup water
3 tablespoons butter or margarine
3 tablespoons brown sugar
½ teaspoon nutmeg
½ teaspoon cinnamon
2 eggs, beaten
½ to ¾ cup cornmeal
¼ cup raisins

In pot over medium flame, bring milk and water to gentle boil. Reduce heat and add margarine, sugar, and spices. Once sugar is dissolved, add eggs, cornmeal, and raisins. Stir. Cover and cook over low flame for 10 minutes. Stir often to keep from sticking.

ORANGE PUDDING

2 oranges, peeled and sliced
1 teaspoon sugar
⅔ cup milk
1 egg yolk
salt (optional)
1 teaspoon cornstarch
1½ tablespoons sugar

Sprinkle 1 teaspoon sugar over oranges in bowl. In pot over medium flame, combine milk, egg yolk, a pinch of salt, cornstarch, and 1½ tablespoons sugar. Stir until mixture thickens. Pour over orange slices. Allow to cool. If you wish, whip egg white until it stiffens, add sugar, and spoon onto pudding.

Here's a favorite of a British friend of mine.

TRIFLE

In a bowl, place ¾ cup fresh strawberries, sliced (blueberries are great, too), and sprinkle with sugar. Place 2 Twinkies, sliced the long way, on top of fruit.

Custard
1 cup milk
2 egg yolks, beaten
2 tablespoons sugar
1 teaspoon cornstarch

Separate eggs and set egg whites aside. In pot over medium flame, combine milk, egg yolks, 2 tablespoons of sugar, and cornstarch. Stir until mixture thickens, but do not boil. Pour over fruit and Twinkies. Allow to cool. If you wish, beat egg whites until stiff and fold in 1 teaspoon of sugar. Spoon on top of trifle.

This unusual combination tastes great after a long day.

MAC'S SURPRISE

½ cup rice, raw
½ cup water
½ cup raisins
1 apple, peeled, cored, and sliced
1 tablespoon brown sugar
½ teaspoon cinnamon
¼ teaspoon nutmeg

In pot over medium flame, combine rice and water and bring to boil. Add raisins and apple. Stir. Cover and cook until rice is tender, about 15 minutes. Remove from flame and add all other ingredients. Stir and set aside for 10 minutes to cool. If you wish, add a little milk and more sugar.

Earlier we talked about steamed vegetables. Well, you can do the same with fruit.

APPLE DELIGHT

2 MacIntosh apples, top half peeled
2 tablespoons raisins
1 tablespoon sugar
cinnamon to taste

Core apples without puncturing bottoms. In bowl, mix sugar and raisins. Stuff each apple with raisin/sugar mixture. Sprinkle cinnamon over top. Pour enough water in pot to reach bottom of steamer. Place apples on steamer. Cover pot and place over medium flame. Allow to steam at least 30 minutes, adding water if needed.

PEARS 'N COTS

Same recipe as above, except substitute fresh pears for apples, diced dried apricots for raisins, and fresh mint leaves (finely diced) for cinnamon.

Creativity is the rule for desserts in a pot. I've discovered that you can stew or cook just about any fruit to make applesauce, pearsauce, or fruit compote quickly and easily. Just chop the basic ingredients, add various spices to taste, and throw in molasses, brown sugar, or white sugar, depending on how you want the dish to look and taste.

DON'S FRUIT COMPOTE

½ cup dried apricots
½ cup raisins
1 6-oz can Mandarin orange slices
1 fresh peach, peeled and cored
3 tablespoons sugar
⅓ cup water

In pot over medium flame, combine all ingredients. Cover and cook at least 20 minutes. Stir often and add water if needed. Sauce should be thick. Serve with sponge cake or fancy cookies.

SPICED APPLESAUCE

3 apples, peeled, cored, and cut in chunks
¼ cup water
2 tablespoons brown sugar
½ teaspoon cinnamon
¼ teaspoon nutmeg

In pot over medium flame, cook apples in water until they fall apart. Remove from heat and stir to make sauce. Add sugar and spices. Tastes great with oatmeal cookies.

THE OVEN

As Monty Python would say, "And now for something completely different." For a trekker, the height of adventuresome cooking can be found in the outdoor oven. That's right, by simply firing up your stove you can operate an open-air kitchen that will challenge your culinary skills and your tastebuds.

Chapter 2 discusses ovens, both homemade and store bought. Both work equally well, and both produce casseroles, roasts, and baked goods in good order. And both keep you on your toes making sure what you're cooking gets roasted or baked, not fried to a crisp.

There are two differences between my homemade oven and a commercial product such as the Outback Oven. First, the coffee-can oven mimics a true oven in that the can is the body of the oven. That means you can cook food such as baked potatoes on the racks inside. The Outback Oven uses a pan-and-lid configuration inside a heat-capturing tent. The tent is the body of the oven, and the pan and lid make a sort of baking vessel. It's hard to cook a baked potato or a soufflé in it.

The other difference is that the Outback Oven is short—about 3 inches from bottom of pan to top of lid. That makes it difficult to cook upright dishes such as stuffed peppers. This oven is great, however, for pizza, biscuits, and combination dishes such as Uncle Ben's Chicken, which I include later in this chapter. And if you're careful, you can use the bottom pan of this oven as a frying pan.

If you choose carefully, you can make almost any one-pan oven recipe in any oven—commercial or homemade.

BREAKFAST

Breakfast from the oven is a bit un-American, since the national tendency is to eat breakfast off the top of the stove. But there are some very satisfying ways to kick off the morning using your oven.

I'm an egg person, so I go for the yolk rather than the straight line.

FRANCOISE'S QUICHE

 1 premade Pillsbury pie crust (folded, very compact, uncooked)
 ¼ cup cheddar cheese, sliced thin
 ⅓ cup ham, diced
 ⅓ cup evaporated milk
 2 eggs,
 salt and pepper to taste
 NOTE: If using the Outback Oven, double all ingredients except crust.

Line your small pot (6" diameter) with pie crust and cut off excess. Spread cheese on bottom and add ham on top of cheese. Beat milk, eggs, salt, and pepper together and pour over ham and cheese. Place in oven on lower rack for 15 to 20 minutes or until filling is firm.

(DON'T) BERN TH' EGGS!

 1 tablespoon margarine
 ⅓ cup Swiss cheese, grated
 ¼ cup evaporated milk
 2 eggs

Warm oven pan over stove and melt margarine. Sprinkle about three-fourths of the cheese on bottom of pan. Break eggs onto the cheese without breaking yolks. Pour milk over and sprinkle with remaining cheese. Place in oven 20 minutes. Serve with hard roll and fresh fruit.

MACINTOSH SURPRISE

2 medium apples
⅓ lb sausage
2 eggs
salt and pepper to taste

Core apples from the top, but don't break through bottom. Using a spoon, hollow out inside of apple to make a little pocket, widening opening at top. Fill about two-thirds full with sausage. Place in oven pan. Break an egg on top of the sausage (sides of apple will hold it in place). Bake in medium oven at least 25 to 30 minutes. Add salt and pepper to taste.

Your eyes will remember this recipe immediately. The odor of onions on your hands will remind you of it all day.

BERMUDA EGGS

1 medium Bermuda onion
2 large eggs
1 tablespoon Parmesan cheese
¼ teaspoon tarragon
2 tablespoons parsley, chopped
2 tablespoons bread crumbs
pepper to taste

Cut onion in half along "equator" (stem and root ends being the poles). Scoop out inner rings of onion, leaving two "cups." Place onion halves in oven pan and break one egg into each. Dice remaining onion and sprinkle on egg. Combine cheese, tarragon, parsley, bread crumbs, and pepper. Place healthy scoop on top of diced onions. Gently smooth to cover entire cavity. Add extra as needed. Cook in medium oven for about 15 minutes or until bread crumbs are browned. For added flavor, sprinkle with diced ham before cooking.

You can also get away from eggs and use your oven to build some truly remarkable creations.

AMSTERDAM APPLE PANCAKE

2 tablespoons margarine
2 tablespoons brown sugar
1 large apple, peeled, cored, and sliced lengthwise
     about ⅛- to ¼-inch thick
⅛ teaspoon cinnamon
1 egg, beaten
¼ cup milk
⅓ cup Bisquick

In oven pan, melt margarine and spread brown sugar evenly on bottom of pan. Layer apple slices on sugar. Sprinkle with cinnamon. Combine egg, milk, and Bisquick and pour batter over fruit and sugar. Bake about 20 minutes in medium oven or until top of pancake is nicely browned. Flip onto plate so brown sugar and apples are on top.

RASHER CAKE

2 eggs, separated
½ cup milk
½ teaspoon sugar
½ cup flour
½ cup white cornmeal
1 teaspoon baking powder
6 slices bacon
pepper to taste

Beat egg yolks until light. Add remaining ingredients except bacon and egg whites. Beat egg whites until stiff. Fold into batter. Fry bacon in pan and drain grease. Pour batter over bacon slices and bake in hot oven 10 minutes. Reduce heat and continue baking until cake is set in center.

LUNCH AND DINNER

The oven offers countless opportunities to put variety into your menu—roasts, cakes, casseroles, pies, bread, snacks, and even pizza. As far as I'm concerned, the oven is the best thing going when it's dinner time.

Poultry

Chicken is one of the easiest meats to cook in the oven but it can also be one of the most boring. So we'll start with the basics and spice it up from there.

BBC (BASIC BAKED CHICKEN)

½ lb chicken (white or dark pieces)
1 medium onion, sliced
1 stalk celery, chopped
1 carrot, cut in strips
1 medium potato, cut in chunks
salt and pepper to taste

Place chicken in oven pan and surround with vegetables. Add salt and pepper. Bake about 45 minutes in medium oven. Serve with a hard roll and fruit.

CUED BIRD

½ cup hot water
1 beef bouillon cube
½ lb of chicken (white or dark pieces)
1 fresh tomato, crushed
1 tablespoon Worcestershire sauce
4 tablespoons ketchup
1 onion, diced
¼ teaspoon dry mustard
1 teaspoon parsley
¼ teaspoon salt (optional)
¼ teaspoon pepper
1 cup precooked rice

Dissolve bouillon cube in hot water. Combine with all other ingredients except chicken and rice to make BBQ sauce. Place chicken in oven pan and pour sauce over chicken. Bake 45 minutes in a medium oven. Add pre-cooked rice to pan 10 minutes before removing dinner from oven.

UNCLE BEN'S CHICKEN

2 chicken breasts, boned
½ cup seasoned bread stuffing
2 tablespoons water
1 cup precooked long grain and wild rice mixture
1 red pepper, cut in strips
1 green pepper, cut in strips
1 carrot, cut in strips

Note: By "2 chicken breasts" we mean one whole breast sliced in half, with the two halves joined to look something like a Valentine heart. Mix stuffing and water. Flatten chicken breasts slightly and spoon about half the stuffing onto breasts. Roll up breasts and secure with toothpick. Place chicken in oven pan. Surround with precooked rice mixture. Lay pepper and carrot over top. Cover and bake 35 to 45 minutes.

"PARDON ME, BUT DO YOU HAVE ANY . . . " CHICKEN

2 chicken breasts, boned (leave skin on)
1 clove garlic, minced
2 tablespoons Dijon mustard
¼ teaspoon thyme
salt and pepper to taste

Mix garlic with mustard, thyme, salt, and pepper. Remove skin gently from meat and rub mixture on chicken. Replace skin and salt and pepper again. Place chicken in oven pan and bake 35 to 40 minutes on low rack. If you like, cut a potato in half, wrap it in foil, and bake it on the higher rack.

GREAT FLAVORED BIRD

1 chicken breast, boned
1 fresh lemon
1 tablespoon dried mustard
1 teaspoon brown sugar
¼ teaspoon pepper
½ teaspoon coriander
1 teaspoon vegetable oil
¾ cup raisins
1 cup precooked noodles

Squeeze lemon and dice about 1 tablespoon of lemon peel. Combine juice, peel, and dry ingredients. Rub oven pan with oil and place chicken in pan. Bake chicken for 15 minutes in medium to high oven (lower rack setting in oven). Brush with sauce mixture, turn in pan, and bake another 15 minutes. Add raisins and remaining sauce. Bake 15 minutes. Serve with precooked noodles.

Up to this point, we've worked with basic variations on baked chicken. Now let's step up our creativity one notch.

UNUSUAL BIRD

1 chicken breast, precooked and diced
1 tablespoon Crisco
2 tablespoons flour
¾ cup milk
1 egg, beaten
½ cup precooked rice
¼ cup cheddar cheese, grated
salt and pepper to taste

In oven pan on stove, melt Crisco and stir in flour, salt, and pepper. Gradually add milk, stirring to keep from burning. Bring to boil. Remove from heat and add egg. Stir until well blended. Add chicken. Cover with layer of rice and then cheese. Bake in medium oven 20 minutes.

CRUMBY CHICKEN

¼ cup milk
½ cup seasoned bread crumbs
¼ cup Parmesan cheese
½ lb chicken (white or dark pieces)
1 yellow squash or zucchini, cut in 1" slices

Mix cheese and bread crumbs. Dip chicken in milk and roll in coating mix. Place in bottom of oven pan. Dip squash in milk and in then in coating mix. Arrange vegetables on top of chicken. Bake in medium oven 45 minutes.

BIG KING CHICKEN CASSEROLE

2 tablespoons butter or margarine
2 tablespoons green pepper, diced
1 small onion, diced
¼ cup mushrooms, sliced
2 tablespoons flour
¾ cup milk
1 egg, beaten
1 tablespoon pimento, sliced thin
pepper to taste
1 chicken breast, precooked and diced
bread crumbs

In oven pan over flame, melt butter or margarine. Brown green pepper, onions, and mushrooms. Add flour and blend. Add milk, egg, pimento, and pepper. Cook until thick. Add chicken. Stir and remove from heat. Cover with layer of bread crumbs and bake 25 minutes or until bread crumbs are browned.

POULET PIE

  ½ lb chicken, precooked and diced
  1-oz packet powdered chicken gravy mix
  1 cup water
  2 prepared pie crusts
  1 carrot, diced
  1 potato, sliced thin
  1 stalk celery, diced

Prepare gravy mix in a metal cup over a medium to low flame according to packet directions. Line oven pan with one pie crust. Mix chicken and vegetables together and put in pie. Pour gravy mix over the top. Cover with other crust, pinching edges to seal. Cut slits in top crust to vent. Bake in medium oven 45 minutes or until pie crust is nicely browned.

CHEESY CHICKEN

  ½ cup Monterey Jack cheese, shredded
  ½ cup milk
  ½ lb chicken breast, precooked and diced
  1 cup precooked macaroni
  1 sweet red pepper, diced
  seasoned bread crumbs

Over medium flame, heat milk to almost boiling. Slowly add cheese and stir until smooth. In oven pan, combine chicken, macaroni, and red pepper. Pour cheese sauce over top. Sprinkle with bread crumbs. Bake in a medium oven 25 minutes.

HULA BIRD

 2 chicken breasts, boned (see note in Uncle Ben's
      Chicken recipe, page 117)
 ⅓ cup freeze-dried green beans, rehydrated
 1 orange, peeled and sliced
 1 small can crushed pineapple
 ¼ teaspoon ginger
 ¼ teaspoon cinnamon
 ½ cup precooked rice

Place chicken breasts in oven pan. Surround with beans. Lay orange slices over top and pour pineapple (including juice) over all. Sprinkle with cinnamon and ginger. Cover with foil (not needed with Outback Oven). Bake 45 minutes in medium to high oven (keep on upper rack, but use higher flame). If there's room in pan, add rice 5 minutes before serving. If not, remove chicken from oven at proper time. Wrap rice in foil and cook on top rack for 5 minutes.

DIVINE CHICKEN

 1 chicken breast, boned
 ¾ cup broccoli
 1 packet mushroom soup mix, reconstituted (single-serving size)

Place chicken breast in oven pan and cover with broccoli. Pour mushroom soup over all. Cover and bake in medium oven 35 to 40 minutes.

Vegetarian Delights

A lot of these recipes can be considered side dishes, snacks, or à la carte fare. But you can make a full meal out of each one if you take the time to think about the four food groups. You can cover a lot of grain with a kaiser roll and a considerable amount of dairy protein with a half cup of cheese. So try making one or more of these a centerpiece in your one-pan feast!

This recipe works best in the Outback Oven because of its wide, flat design.

THE ONE-PAN PIZZA

1 package pizza dough mix
1 tablespoon olive oil
1 large tomato, chopped
¼ cup mushrooms, sliced
salt to taste
½ teaspoon oregano
½ teaspoon fresh basil
½ cup mozzarella cheese, shredded

Prepare dough according to package directions. Flatten dough to 10-inch diameter. Rub with olive oil. Sprinkle with tomatoes and then layer with mushrooms. Sprinkle with salt and spices and top with final layer of cheese. Bake in very hot oven about 10 to 15 minutes. If you crave meat, add sausage or sliced pepperoni before the cheese.

JOHN BARLEY CAKE

¼ cup flour
1¼ cups water
½ cup barley, raw
1 medium onion, diced
1 medium zucchini, diced
½ tablespoon vegetable oil
¼ teaspoon salt (optional)
¼ teaspoon oregano

Mix flour with ¾ cup water; stir to remove lumps.
Combine with remaining ingredients (including remaining
½ cup water) in oven pan. Cook in medium oven 30 minutes or until water is absorbed and top is firm.

You can try this to add a special touch to your camp
table.

A-MAIZE-ING SOUFFLÉ

1 tablespoon butter or margarine
1 tablespoon flour
¾ cup corn
2 eggs
1 cup hot milk
1 teaspoon salt (optional)
pepper and paprika to taste

Blend butter and flour. To this, add corn, milk, salt, pepper, and paprika. Separate eggs and beat yolks until light;
add to mixture. Beat egg whites until stiff and fold into
mixture. Cook in medium-hot oven about 1 hour.

From this delicate taste treat, you could go all-
American—or at least all-Wisconsin.

MACARONI AND CHEESE MOM'S WAY

½ cup milk
¾ cup Monterey Jack cheese, shredded
1½ cups macaroni, precooked
⅓ cup seasoned bread crumbs

Over medium flame, heat the milk until it almost boils.
Gradually add ½ cup of cheese, stirring so it doesn't burn.
Once sauce is ready, pour over macaroni in oven pan.
Sprinkle with remaining cheese and then with bread
crumbs. Cook in medium oven 25 to 30 minutes or until
bread crumbs are toasty brown.

NO-NOODLE LASAGNA

  1 small to medium eggplant, cut in ¼" slices
  salt to taste
  1 egg
  ¼ cup milk
  ¼ cup olive oil
  ½ cup seasoned bread crumbs
  1 cup spaghetti sauce
  8 oz provolone cheese, sliced

Sprinkle eggplant with salt (if desired) and set aside on towel to drain for 10 minutes. Then rinse. Beat egg with milk. Heat oil in pan over medium flame. Dip eggplant in egg mixture and then into bread crumbs. Brown both sides. Set on towel to drain. Build stacks of eggplant, sauce, and cheese. Bake in medium oven 25 to 30 minutes. Adjust number of stacks and layers per stack to suit oven dimensions.

HAM 'N CHEESE SPUDS

  3 medium potatoes, sliced thin
  1 medium onion, sliced thin
  4 oz ham, diced (optional)
  ⅓ cup cheddar cheese, grated
  ¾ cup milk
  2 tablespoons flour
  salt and pepper to taste

In oven pan, layer potatoes with ham, cheese, and onion. Combine milk, flour, salt, and pepper. Pour over mixture in pan. Bake in medium oven 45 minutes.

PEPPERS À LA SHROOM

2 medium green peppers
¾ cup mushrooms, sliced
1 medium tomato, chopped
½ cup mozzarella cheese, grated
½ teaspoon oregano
¼ teaspoon fennel seed
bread crumbs

Cut tops off peppers and clean out seeds. Combine mushrooms, tomato, cheese, oregano, and fennel. Stuff peppers. Sprinkle bread crumbs over the top and cook in medium oven (control heat by flame because you might have to use the lower rack to accommodate height of peppers) 30 to 45 minutes.

Sticking with stuffed vegetables for a moment. . . .

FULL-HOUSE MUSHROOMS

4 to 6 very large mushrooms
1 small onion, minced
¼ cup fresh spinach leaves, minced
2 teaspoons olive oil
½ teaspoon basil
¼ teaspoon salt (optional)
¼ teaspoon pepper
1 tablespoon Parmesan cheese
2 tablespoons bread crumbs

Remove stems from mushrooms. Mince those and combine with remaining ingredients. If mixture doesn't stick together, add more bread crumbs. Stuff each cap tightly, leaving a mound ½ inch or so above edge of cap. Lay in oven pan and bake in hot oven 10 minutes or until stuffing begins to brown.

ART-I-CHOKE ON THESE TOMATOES?

1 large tomato
2 marinated artichoke hearts
1 teaspoon olive oil
3 tablespoons seasoned bread crumbs
2 thick slices provolone cheese
2 jumbo green olives stuffed with pimento

Cut tomato in half. Out of each half, scoop a hole just large enough to hold one artichoke heart. Mix oil with bread crumbs and press a handful on top of each tomato half. Bake in medium oven 20 minutes. Lay slice of cheese on top and complete with olive on top of that. Bake another 5 minutes or until cheese melts (but does not run or burn).

Packed with protein, calcium, B vitamins, and fiber, this meal will keep you full for hours. The beans and rice provide protein complementation and the cheese and cottage cheese supply additional protein.

CHEESY BEANS AND RICE

1½ cups brown rice, precooked
½ can kidney beans, drained and repackaged
1 clove garlic, minced
1 medium onion, chopped
1 4-oz can chopped green chili peppers
4 oz shredded cheese
1 cup low-fat cottage cheese
½ cup (2 oz) grated sharp cheddar cheese

In bowl, combine rice, beans, garlic, onion, and chili peppers. Layer this mixture alternately with shredded cheese and cottage cheese in an oiled pan. End with a layer of the bean-rice mixture. Bake in medium oven 30 minutes. During the last few minutes of baking, sprinkle sharp cheddar cheese on top.

Here's a great lunch recipe to serve hot or cold; I usually make it ahead of time and serve it cold with a fruit salad. This recipe is very high in protein, iron, calcium, vitamin A, and beta-carotene. It is also relatively low in fat since there is no pie crust. If you don't like spinach, you can substitute broccoli.

CRUSTLESS SPINACH PIE

1 package (10 oz) frozen chopped spinach or broccoli, thawed and well drained (or use fresh spinach or broccoli, cooked, well drained, and chopped)
½ lb sharp cheddar or feta cheese, grated or crumbled
2 cups low-fat cottage cheese
4 eggs
6 tablespoons flour
¼ teaspoon salt
½ teaspoon pepper

In a bowl, combine spinach, grated cheese, and cottage cheese. In a cup, mix eggs with a fork and add flour, salt, and pepper. Combine both mixtures and mix well. Place mixture in a lightly oiled or nonstick-sprayed pie pan, and bake 1 hour in medium oven.

Of course, you can also use your oven simply to bake vegetables.

SOLID SQUASH SURPRISE

1 small acorn squash (1 to 1½ lb)
1 orange, peeled and halved
2 tablespoons brown sugar
2 tablespoons margarine

Cut squash in half along the equator. Clean out seeds. Trim ends so that the halves do not roll onto their sides. Push half of orange into each cavity, enlarging the cavity as needed. Divide sugar and margarine evenly and place on top of orange. Cover trimmed ends with foil. Bake in hot oven 40 minutes or until squash is tender.

Beef

Here's where the trail oven can make a big difference in a trekker's life. The land of roasts, of exciting combinations of richly flavored meats and interesting sauces, will come to life as you light up your life and your stove.

The wide variety of cuts available to the outdoor chef make beef a versatile choice. Whether you decide to use hamburger or steak, there's always something fun to cook. Remember, though, that beef can be fatty, gristly, tough, or all of the above. Cooks, both famous and mundane, have found ways to turn inexpensive beef into toothsome meals fit for lord and lady.

SHEPHERD'S PIE

2 large potatoes, peeled and sliced thin
2 tablespoons butter or margarine
¼ cup milk
½ lb ground beef
salt and pepper to taste
2 tablespoons flour
¼ cup water
2 carrots, chopped
1 stalk celery, chopped
1 medium onion, chopped

Using your oven pan as a pot, place potatoes in salted water and boil 15 minutes. Drain water. Mash potatoes with butter and milk. Remove from pan and set aside. Clean pan. Over medium flame, brown hamburger until crumbly. Reduce heat, and add salt, pepper, flour, and water. Stir to make gravy. Remove from heat. Add vegetables and stir to mix. Make crust of mashed potatoes over the top of the meat-and-vegetable mixture. Bake 35 minutes.

DEEP-DISH STEAK

½ lb round steak, cut 1½" thick
¼ cup flour
1 teaspoon salt (optional)
¼ teaspoon pepper
1½ tablespoons vegetable oil
1 medium onion, chopped
1 green pepper, chopped
1 stalk celery, chopped
¼ cup raisins
2 medium tomatoes, cut in chunks

Mix flour, salt, and pepper. Rub into steak. Heat oven pan over medium flame. Add oil and brown meat on both sides. Remove from heat. Add remaining ingredients. Cover and bake in medium oven 1 to 1½ hours. Turn meat every once in a while. Serve with bread.

A DIFFERENT SORT OF ONION

1 large onion
¼ lb each ground beef and ground pork
¼ cup salted peanuts, chopped
¼ teaspoon pepper
⅛ teaspoon nutmeg
1 beef bouillon cube
1 cup water
1 8-oz can whole tomatoes
¼ cup mushrooms, chopped
2 tablespoons each sour cream and Madeira wine

Cut onion in half and remove center (save), leaving two "cups." Mix beef, pork, nuts, pepper, and nutmeg. Stuff onion halves. Place in oven pan. Dissolve bouillon cube in water and pour into pan with half of tomatoes. Bake in medium oven 1 hour. While main dish is cooking, mince onion centers. Combine mushrooms, onions, remaining tomatoes, sour cream, and wine in metal cup and heat on stove to make sauce. Pour over the onion halves prior to serving.

DON CARLOS'S STEAK SURPRISE

½ lb top round steak, cut in strips
¼ cup green onion, chopped
1 green pepper, sliced
1 large tomato, chopped
1 clove garlic, minced
1 tablespoon olive oil
1 teaspoon chili powder
½ teaspoon salt (optional)

In oven pan over medium flame, sauté vegetables in oil until tender. Add meat. Remove from heat. Add seasonings and stir until well coated. Cover and bake in medium oven 35 to 40 minutes.

MERRY-NADE POT ROAST

½ lb chuck steak or Boston roast
2 tablespoons Italian salad dressing
2 tablespoons margarine
½ cup water
1 medium onion, sliced
2 carrots, sliced
1 large potato, cut in chunks
1 tablespoon margarine
2 tablespoons water
1 teaspoon flour

Rub salad dressing over meat. In oven pan, melt 2 tablespoons margarine over medium flame and brown meat. Remove from heat and add water and vegetables. Bake in medium oven 1 hour. Remove meat from pan and add 1 tablespoon margarine. Combine flour and water and stir into sauce to thicken gravy.

Staying Italian for a moment. . . .

KATIE'S LASAGNA

6 to 8 oz lasagna noodles, precooked
½ lb ground round
1 cup spaghetti sauce
½ cup ricotta cheese
¼ cup Parmesan cheese

Brown beef in pan, drain, and add spaghetti sauce. Remove from pan. Place single layer of noodles on bottom of pan. Combine cheeses in bowl. Top with layer of cheese, followed by layer of meat sauce. Repeat until you run out of noodles. (You might have to cut noodles in half to accommodate reduced pan size.) Bake in medium oven 35 to 40 minutes.

SAUCY BEEF

½ lb top or bottom round
salt and pepper to taste
2 tablespoons flour
1 tablespoon prepared mustard
1 tablespoon vegetable oil
1 medium onion, diced
1 large potato, sliced thin
1 beef bouillon cube
1 cup hot water
¼ cup sour cream

Rub flour onto meat. Season with salt and pepper. Rub mustard on meat. Cut into bite-sized chunks. Heat oil in oven pan and brown meat. Add onions and sauté until tender. Remove from heat and dissolve bouillon cube in water. Pour over meat. Add potatoes. Bake in medium oven 45 minutes. Just before serving, add sour cream to create an incredible sauce. Serve with fresh carrot sticks and rolls.

RED-EYE STEW

½ lb stew beef, cut in small cubes
1 tablespoon margarine
1 medium onion, chopped
½ teaspoon salt (optional)
1 teaspoon paprika
¼ teaspoon caraway seeds
1 6-oz can tomato paste
1 beef bouillon cube dissolved in 1 cup hot water
2 medium potatoes, cubed

In oven pan, melt margarine over medium flame and brown beef. Reduce heat and sauté onions. Remove from heat and add all ingredients except potatoes. Cover and bake 1 hour in medium oven. Add potatoes and cook another 30 minutes. Serve with hard rolls.

Stepping up your meat selection a notch can bring even more interesting taste variations. By purchasing sirloin, eye of round, and filet, you'll be putting four-star restaurant quality on your outdoor table.

BIG BEN BEEF BAKE

½ lb flank steak
2 tablespoons honey
2 tablespoons BBQ sauce
1 tablespoon vegetable oil
1 tablespoon lemon juice
1 large onion, cut in chunks
1 red pepper, sliced

Combine honey, BBQ sauce, oil, and lemon juice to make a sauce. Rub into meat and let meat rest in sauce 10 to 15 minutes. Place meat in oven pan and surround with vegetables. Pour sauce over all. Bake 15 to 20 minutes in medium to hot oven. Serve with reheated noodles.

RIB-EYE ECSTASY

½ lb rib-eye steak
1 tablespoon vegetable oil
½ teaspoon each salt (optional) and pepper
½ teaspoon paprika
¼ teaspoon garlic powder
1 medium onion, sliced
½ cup rehydrated corn, drained

Combine seasonings. Rub both sides of steak with oil and seasonings. Lay onion on bottom of oven pan and place meat on top. Cover and bake in hot oven 20 minutes. After 15 minutes, spoon corn onto meat. You can add a little steak sauce after cooking, if you like.

BBQ BRISKET

½ lb beef brisket
½ cup BBQ sauce
1 medium onion, sliced

Rub sauce into meat and let stand 30 minutes. Place in oven pan with onions and sauce. Cover and bake in low to medium oven for 1 to 1½ hours. Slice across grain and serve on hard roll or with rice, accompanied by fresh fruit and carrots.

BARON BEEF

½ lb eye-of-round roast
1 tablespoon vegetable oil
1 tablespoon Kitchen Bouquet
1 teaspoon each salt (optional), pepper, and thyme

Combine oil and Kitchen Bouquet. Rub over meat. Mix salt, pepper, and thyme and rub over meat. Place roast in oven pan. Bake 15 minutes in very hot oven. Reduce heat and continue baking for another hour. On top rack of oven, cook a baked potato (foil wrapped, potato cut in half).

CAP O' FILET (IT'S THE TOP!)
- 2 filets mignon (about 1½" thick)
- 2 tablespoons liver paté
- 1 tablespoon olive oil
- 1 teaspoon celery salt (optional)
- 2 large mushrooms
- ¼ cup Gruyère cheese, grated
- 2 tablespoons fresh spinach, minced
- 2 tablespoons seasoned bread crumbs
- 1 teaspoon olive oil
- 2 slices Gruyère cheese (¼" thick)

In each filet, make a pocket by cutting into side; be careful not to cut filet in half. Stuff cavity with 1 tablespoon of paté (should not squirt out edge). Rub oil on meat and season with celery salt. Set aside. Mix grated cheese, spinach, bread crumbs, and oil. Remove stem of mushrooms. Carefully cut off part of cap to make flat surface. Stuff mushrooms with cheese mixture. Place meat in oven pan and bake in medium oven about 20 minutes. Place one slice of cheese and one mushroom on top of each filet and continue baking another 10 minutes.

Pork, Ham, and Other Ovenables

Ovens make a big difference in the way you eat when trekking. Take pork, for example. Sure, you can fry a chop or dice up some loin and mix it with veggies. But imagine the lip smacking that will go on when you fire up the oven and make a mess of ribs or pork roast smothered in applesauce. Think about how good your stomach will feel when you wrap yourself around a mouth-watering casserole that highlights ham and cheese. Remember to cook your pork thoroughly! Enough thinking. How about some eating?

CORTLAND PORK ROAST

½ lb boneless pork loin roast
1 tablespoon vegetable oil
1 tablespoon brown sugar
1 medium apple, chopped
½ cup applesauce
2 tablespoons brown sugar
1 teaspoon cinnamon
1 teaspoon nutmeg

Rub oil and then 1 tablespoon brown sugar onto roast. Bake in a medium oven 45 minutes. Combine apple, applesauce, 2 tablespoons brown sugar, and spices. Spoon over roast. Cover and bake another 45 minutes. Serve with reheated rice and relish tray of pickles, olives, pickled beets, and celery.

CHAMPIGNON CHOPS

2 center-cut loin chops, boned
1 packet mushroom soup (single-serving size) and water
    to prepare
parsley, chopped
1 large potato, sliced

In oven pan, brown chops in a little oil. Remove from heat and pour mushroom soup over top. Sprinkle with parsley. Lay potato around edge of pan. Cover and bake 45 minutes in medium oven.

MOM'S TUNA-NOODLE CASSEROLE

1 cup egg noodles, precooked
1 tablespoon vegetable oil
1 can tuna, drained
1 packet mushroom soup mix (single-serving size) and
    water to prepare
¼ cup parsley, chopped
1 tablespoon margarine, melted
bread crumbs

In lightly greased oven pan, mix tuna, noodles, soup, and parsley. Drizzle melted margarine over top. Sprinkle bread crumbs over all. Bake 35 minutes in medium oven.

ITALIAN SAUSAGE BAKE-OFF

½ lb mild Italian sausage
1 8-oz can tomato sauce
¼ teaspoon oregano
¼ teaspoon basil
¼ teaspoon garlic powder
1 teaspoon sugar
1 bay leaf
¼ teaspoon fennel seed
1 teaspoon Parmesan cheese
1 medium onion, chopped
1 large green pepper, sliced
1 zucchini, sliced
3 slices provolone cheese

In oven pan, brown sausage. In bowl, mix tomato sauce, seasonings, sugar, and Parmesan to make marinara sauce. Remove pan from heat and add vegetables. Pour sauce over all. Lay slices of provolone cheese over top and bake in hot oven 35 to 40 minutes. Serve over precooked pasta. Add a diced tomato, if you wish.

Here's an easy meal that will fill you up.

BIG BBQ RIBS

2 farmer-style (i.e., with meat on, not spare ribs) pork ribs
½ cup BBQ sauce
1 medium onion, cut in chunks
1 cup rice, precooked

In oven pan, place ribs and smother with BBQ sauce. Pack onions around ribs. Bake in medium oven 45 minutes to 1 hour. About 10 minutes before ribs are done, add rice.

LANAI GROUND LOIN

½ lb ground pork loin
½ teaspoon salt (optional)
1 small Vidalia (sweet) onion, diced
1 sweet red pepper, diced
¼ teaspoon dry mustard
1 egg, beaten
½ cup bread crumbs
½ cup crushed pineapple

Combine all ingredients. Turn into lightly greased oven pan and bake in medium oven 45 minutes. Serve with fresh sliced summer squash.

YAM 'N HAM

½ lb smoked shoulder or canned ham
whole cloves
2 tablespoons brown sugar
1 medium sweet potato, quartered
2 tablespoons margarine

Place meat in oven pan. Stud ham with cloves and sprinkle with brown sugar. Place sweet potato around meat with skin side down. Dab margarine on each sweet potato. Cover and bake in medium oven 75 minutes. Serve with reheated rice.

PORK PIE (NO HAT)

1 package prepared pie crust (2 crusts)
1 cup pork loin, precooked and diced
¼ cup bacon bits
1 large potato, sliced thin
1 medium onion, diced
brown gravy mix and 1 cup water to prepare
salt and pepper to taste
½ teaspoon sage

Line oven pan with one pie crust. Sprinkle with bacon bits. Layer potatoes and onions. Mix salt, pepper, sage, and pork and make a final layer. Pour gravy over all and cover with second pie crust. Pinch edges and cut a few vents in top. Bake in medium oven 1 hour.

SMOKEHOUSE SPECIAL

1 cup ham, diced
2 medium potatoes, peeled and sliced thin
1 medium onion, sliced
½ cup cheddar cheese
½ cup milk
2 tablespoons flour
2 to 3 tablespoons bread crumbs

In oven pan, heat milk to near boiling and add cheese and flour to make sauce. Remove from heat and add ham, potatoes, and onions. Stir to mix well. Sprinkle bread crumbs over the top and bake in medium oven 45 minutes.

Baked Goods

With an oven in hand, you can make bread, rolls, and biscuits. You can also bake cakes and pies, but look for those under "Desserts," below.

A lot of the prepackaged rolls you buy will keep a day or two without refrigeration. Simply pack the cylinder near your frozen meat to keep it cool until you're ready to bake them. Then follow package instructions.

If you're a bit more ambitious, you can start from scratch. There's been a lot written about in-camp breads, so I'll include only my favorites here.

BIG D'S BISCUITS

½ cup flour
½ teaspoon baking powder
pinch of salt (optional)
1 teaspoon vegetable oil
¼ cup water

Combine all ingredients, adding just enough water to make a good stiff dough. Flour your hands and make biscuits about 2 inches in diameter and 1 inch thick. Place on greased oven pan. Bake 10 to 15 minutes, checking to see that biscuits don't burn.

HI-HO CORN BREAD

¾ cup flour
⅓ cup yellow cornmeal
2 tablespoons sugar
salt (optional)
1 teaspoon baking powder
1 egg, beaten
½ cup milk
2 tablespoons vegetable oil

Mix dry ingredients. Add wet ingredients, stirring to mix batter evenly. Pour batter in greased oven pan and bake 25 minutes in a hot oven. Check to make sure bread doesn't burn.

This next recipe works great in a frying pan, too. Simply cook the patties 2 to 3 minutes per side or until browned.

HUSH MY PUPPIES

1 cup yellow cornmeal
½ teaspoon salt (optional)
½ teaspoon baking powder
1 egg, beaten
½ cup milk
1 tablespoon onion, minced
1 tablespoon vegetable oil

Combine dry ingredients. Add egg, milk, and onion. Mix together to form dough. Shape into ½-inch oblong patties and place on oven pan. Brush tops and bottoms with oil and bake in hot oven 10 to 15 minutes or until nicely browned.

SHORTCAKE BISCUITS

1 cup flour
1½ teaspoons baking powder
1½ tablespoons sugar
¼ teaspoon salt (optional)
1 egg, beaten
⅓ cup milk
2 tablespoons vegetable oil

Combine all ingredients and mix (will be stiff). If dough seems too loose, add flour as needed. Coat hands with flour and make biscuits about ½- to ¾-inch thick and 3 inches across. Bake in hot oven 15 minutes.

DESSERT

Do you like dessert? The oven is the way to go for after-dinner tasties. Any cake mix will do for starters, and brownies fill you up after a long day of trekking. And all of these come in prepackaged, ready-to-go form. Just visit the baking aisle at your store.

If you're planning to use a commercial cake mix, remember that you have to watch oven temperature. One-pan ovens can leave you with a charred "might have been." Test for doneness with a toothpick. Stick it in the middle of the cake. If it comes out clean, the cake is done.

The following recipes work well outdoors, both when you're cooking and when you're eating.

POWERFUL GINGERBREAD

¼ cup margarine
¼ cup sugar
1 egg, beaten
1 cup flour
½ teaspoon baking soda
½ teaspoon cinnamon
½ teaspoon ginger
¼ teaspoon ground cloves
¼ teaspoon salt (optional)
⅓ cup molasses
½ cup hot water
¼ cup raisins

Cream margarine and sugar in a bowl using fork. Add egg. Combine dry ingredients in a cup or bowl. Mix molasses and hot water in a cup. Alternate adding dry ingredients and molasses mixture to sugar and egg. Beat until smooth. Stir in raisins. Pour into greased oven pan and bake in medium oven 45 minutes.

APPLE HEAVEN

2 medium apples (MacIntosh are best), sliced thin
2 tablespoons brown sugar
2 teaspoons margarine
½ teaspoon cinnamon
½ teaspoon nutmeg

Place apples in oven pan. Sprinkle with brown sugar and spices and place dots of margarine all around. Cover and bake in medium oven 20 minutes.

APPLE-CINNAMON COFFEE CAKE

Cake
1¼ cup Bisquick
½ cup applesauce
¼ cup brown sugar
2 teaspoons cinnamon
¼ cup milk
1 egg, beaten

Topping
½ cup brown sugar
2 tablespoons margarine

Lightly mix brown sugar, cinnamon, milk, and egg. Gradually add Bisquick until you have a smooth batter. Pour into greased oven pan. Mix topping ingredients together until crumbly. Sprinkle over top of batter. Bake in medium oven 25 minutes or until center of coffee cake is done.

BLUE-TOOTH COBBLER

½ cup blueberries (substitute apples, sliced thin, if
    desired)
½ teaspoon cinnamon
¼ teaspoon nutmeg
½ teaspoon flour
1 cup Bisquick
2 tablespoons margarine
¼ cup sugar
1 egg, beaten
½ cup milk

In oven pan, combine blueberries, spices, and flour. In bowl, mix all other ingredients and pour over fruit mixture. Bake in medium oven 25 minutes or until top is browned.

TWOTI-FRUITI PIE

1 package prepared pie crust (2 crusts)
½ cup blueberries
¾ cup apples, sliced thin
¼ cup sugar
½ teaspoon cinnamon
¼ teaspoon nutmeg
1 teaspoon flour
1 tablespoon margarine

Place one pie crust in bottom of oven pan. In bowl, mix fruit and all other ingredients except margarine. Pour into crust. Dot top with margarine and cover with top crust. Pinch edges and cut vents in top. Sprinkle top crust with a few drops of water. Bake in medium oven 45 minutes
NOTE: This can also be used as a recipe for apple pie; just double the amount of apples.

Menu Planning

When you plan your trail menu, the first step is to decide whether you feel like eating pot, pan, or oven food, or (if you've got companions to share the cookware load) some combination thereof. Here are three possible menus and associated shopping lists for a modest weekend outing—reaching the trailhead after dinner Friday, heading home after Sunday breakfast. Build from there for longer trips.

FRYING PAN

Saturday
Breakfast: Vegetable Eggs
Lunch: Parmy Shrooms 'n Noodles
Dinner: Chicken Scallopine
Snacks and Desserts: Apples, Oranges

Sunday
Breakfast: Huevos and Tacos

SHOPPING LIST

Carbos	**Protein**	**Vegetables**
tortillas	6 eggs	1 avocado
spaghetti	⅓ lb. ham	2 potatoes
egg noodles	½ lb. chicken breast	7 whole mushrooms
		1 green pepper
		2 onions
		1 clove garlic

Fruits
apples
oranges

Etcetera
red wine, Parmesan cheese, muenster cheese, black olives, chicken bouillon cubes, powdered milk

Spices and Oils
Tabasco sauce, olive oil, corn oil, peanut oil, sugar, flour

Repackage meat, cheeses, milk (if required), and flour. Precook noodles and spaghetti and repackage.

POT

Saturday
Breakfast: Eggs á la Goldenrod
Lunch: Fast Pea Soup
Dinner: Pedro's Rice
Dessert: Indian Pudding
Snacks: Oranges

Sunday
Breakfast: Soy Sauce Steak Sunrise
Hard-Boiled Eggs

SHOPPING LIST

Carbos	Protein	Vegetables
7-grain bread	6 eggs	freeze-dried peas
flour	¼ lb. sirloin	1 carrot
rice	½ lb. burger	1 green pepper
yellow corn meal	¼ lb. ham	3 plum tomatoes
		1 onion

Fruits
oranges
raisins

Etcetera
1 can condensed milk, powdered milk, honey and brown
sugar, crackers

Spices & Oils
soy sauce, thyme, chili powder, nutmeg, cinnamon, white
pepper, margarine

Repackage meat, milk powder (as needed), corn meal,
flour, and bread.
*Note: Many of the spices you purchase can be repackaged
into 35 mm film canisters to build your spice kit.*

OVEN

Saturday
Breakfast: Amsterdam Apple Pancake
Lunch: Beef Stick, Cheese, Bread, Carrots
Dinner: Ham and Cheese Spuds
Dessert: Blue Tooth Cobbler
Snack: Cashews and Raisins

Sunday
Breakfast: Bermuda Eggs

SHOPPING LIST

Carbos	**Protein**	**Vegetables**
Bisquick	4 eggs	1 Bermuda onion
7-grain bread	⅓ lb. beef stick	3 potatoes
flour	¼ lb. ham	1 onion
bread crumbs		1 carrot
		parsley

Fruits and Nuts
apples
blueberries
raisins
cashews

Etcetera
brown sugar, sugar, Parmesan cheese, powdered milk,
cheddar cheese

Spice and Oils
margarine, cinnamon, tarragon, nutmeg

Weights and Measures

Weight
1 ounce (oz.) = 28.35 grams (g)
1 pound (lb.) = 16 ounces = 453.6 grams
2.2 pounds = 1 kilogram (kg)

Capacity (U.S. liquid measure)
1 gill = 4 ounces = 0.1 liter (l)
1 pint (pt.) = 4 gills = 0.5 liter (l)
1 quart (qt.) = 2 pints = 0.9 liter
1 gallon (gal.) = 4 quarts = 3.8 liters

Capacity (British imperial liquid and dry measure)
1 gill = 5 ounces = 142 cubic centimeters (cc) = 0.142 liter
1 pint = 4 gills = 568 cubic centimeters = 0.568 liter
1 quart = 2 pints = 1.1 liters
1 gallon = 4 quarts = 4.5 liters

Thermometer
0° centigrade (Celsius) (C) = 32° Fahrenheit (F)
100°C = 212°F
To convert Fahrenheit to centigrade, deduct 32, multiply by 5, and divide by 9.
To convert centigrade to Fahrenheit, multiply by 9, divide by 5, and add 32.

Sample Menu Form
(Photocopy)

DAY 1_____   **PAGE #**

Dinner

_____   _____

_____   _____

_____   _____

DAY 2_____

Breakfast

_____   _____

_____   _____

Lunch

_____   _____

_____   _____

Dinner

_____   _____

_____   _____

_____   _____

DAY 3_____

Breakfast

_____   _____

_____   _____

Nutritional Content of Some Common Foods

FOOD	KILOCALORIES PER 3.5 OUNCES	%FAT	%PROTEIN	%CARBO-HYDRATE
Dairy products, fats, and oils				
Margarine	720	81.0	0.6	0.4
Low-fat spread	366	36.8	6.0	3.0
Vegetable oil	900	100.0	—	—
Instant dried skim milk	355	1.3	36.0	53.0
Cheddar cheese	398	32.2	25.0	2.1
Edam cheese	305	23.0	24.0	—
Parmesan cheese	410	30.0	35.0	—
Eggs, dried	592	41.2	47.0	4.1
Low-fat cheese spread	175	9.0	20.0	4.0
Dried fruit				
Apples	275	—	1.0	78.0
Apricots	261	—	5.0	66.5
Dates	275	—	2.2	72.9
Figs	275	—	4.3	69.1
Peaches	261	—	3.1	68.3
Raisins	289	—	2.5	77.4

FOOD	KILOCALORIES PER 3.5 OUNCES	%FAT	%PROTEIN	%CARBO-HYDRATE
Vegetables				
Potatoes, dehydrated	352	—	8.3	80.4
Tomato flakes	342	—	10.8	76.7
Baked beans	123	2.6	6.1	19.0
Nuts				
Almonds	600	57.7	18.6	19.5
Brazil nuts	652	66.9	14.3	10.9
Coconut, desiccated	605	62.0	6.0	6.0
Peanut butter	589	49.4	27.8	17.2
Peanuts, roasted	582	49.8	26.0	18.8
Grain products				
Oatmeal	375	7.0	11.0	62.4
Muesli, sweetened	348	6.3	10.4	66.6
Pasta, white	370	—	12.5	75.2
Pasta, whole wheat	323	0.5	12.5	67.2
Rice, brown	359	—	7.5	77.4
Rice, white	363	—	6.7	80.4
Flour, plain	360	2.0	11.0	75.0
Flour, wholemeal	345	3.0	12.0	72.0
Baked products				
Granola bar	382	13.4	4.9	64.4
Crispbread, rye	345	1.2	13.0	76.3
Oat crackers	369	15.7	10.1	65.6
Bread, white	271	—	8.7	50.5
Bread, wholemeal	243	—	10.5	47.7
Cookies, chocolate	525	28.0	6.0	67.0
Fig bar	356	5.6	3.9	75.4
Cake, fruit	355	13.0	5.0	58.0

FOOD	KILOCALORIES PER 3.5 OUNCES	%FAT	%PROTEIN	%CARBO-HYDRATE
Meat and fish				
Beef, dried	204	6.3	34.3	—
Beef, corned, canned	264	18.0	23.5	—
Salami	490	45.0	19.0	2.0
Salmon, canned	151	7.1	20.8	—
Sardines, drained	165	11.1	24.0	—
Tuna, drained	165	8.2	28.8	—
Sugars and sweets				
Honey	303	—	0.3	82.0
Sugar, brown	373	—	—	96.4
Sugar, white	384	—	—	99.5
Chocolate (milk)	518	32.3	7.7	56.9
Custard, instant	378	10.2	2.9	72.6
Drinks				
Cocoa, mix	391	10.6	9.4	73.9
Coffee	2	—	0.2	—
Tea	1	—	0.1	—

Adapted from Agricultural Handbook No. 8: Composition of Foods *(U.S. Department of Agriculture);* Food Facts *by David Briggs and Mark Wahlquist; and manufacturer's specifications. Courtesy of* The Backpacker's Handbook *by Chris Townsend (Ragged Mountain Press, 1993)*

Index

The One Pan Gourmet Recipe Contest

Have a favorite one-pan, one-pot, or oven recipe that uses fresh foods and has proved itself on the trail? Send it along to Ragged Mountain Press. If it's published in a subsequent edition of *The One Pan Gourmet*, we'll include your byline and send you a free copy of the book. Please print or type your recipe and send it to:

One-Pan Recipe Contest
c/o Ragged Mountain Press
P.O. Box 220
Camden, ME 04843

Receipt of recipes will be acknowledged, but publication cannot be guaranteed.

If you enjoyed *The One Pan Gourmet*, you may be interested in these Ragged Mountain Press books. (Prices are subject to change without notice.)

Shooting Outdoor Videos by Donald C. Steffens

While the compressed scale and neutral lighting of indoor venues may enable most of us to obtain recognizable if not exactly artistic pictures, the vastness, dazzle, and constantly changing aspect of the outdoors quickly expose the misguided weekend artist's attempts for what they are—a waste of good tape and a trap for the unwary attendee of a home-movie screening. Now there is an antidote. *Shooting Outdoor Videos* will help even the most inept among us produce videos worth sharing, whether the subject is flowers, birds, or a child's first soccer game. Paperbound, 128 pages, 50 illustrations (including 10 four-color photos), $12.95.

Fishing and Thinking by A. A. Luce

"Fishing and Thinking is, in my view, the most brilliant book on the subject ever written."
—Patrick Tyner, *Salmon and Trout Magazine*

The fishing that Luce describes is angling for salmon, sea trout, and brown trout on the streams, rivers, tarns, and lakes of Ireland. The thinking ranges from angling problems proper to the weightier matters about which we all at some time ponder. Luce includes notes on the history of places he has fished, on boatcraft, and on the effects of hydroelectric dams on salmon runs, and studies in the cause of the "rise" and the "take." *Fishing and Thinking* makes fascinating and thought-provoking reading, and will be readily identified with by any angler who has sat beside a river, or in an armchair at home, and allowed his or her mind to wander. Hardbound, 208 pages, 12 illustrations, $16.95.